Lauri's Low-Carb Cookbook

Rapid Weight Loss with Satisfying Meals

2nd Edition
Revised

A collection of recipes by:
Lauri Ann Randolph

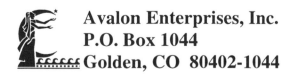

Avalon Enterprises, Inc.
P.O. Box 1044
Golden, CO 80402-1044

Lauri's Low-Carb Cookbook
Rapid Weight Loss
With Satisfying Meals

By Lauri Ann Randolph

Published by:

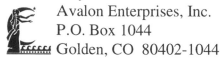 Avalon Enterprises, Inc.
P.O. Box 1044
Golden, CO 80402-1044

1st Edition Copyright © 1999: Cookbooks by Morris Press
First Printing, 1999
Second Printing, 1999

2nd Edition Copyright © 1999: Avalon Enterprises, Inc.
First Printing,1999; completely revised
Second Printing, 2000; revised

ISBN 0-9667963-1-4

Cover Design by Kristin Doughty

Printed in U.S.A by:

Eastwood Printing
2901 Blake Street
Denver, Colorado 80205

**This book is dedicated to
my dear friend Suzan
for her constant support, encouragement
and recipe ideas.**

ABOUT THIS EDITION

The first edition of *Lauri's Low-Carb Cookbook* was a limited edition to test the market demand for such a cookbook. Due to its overwhelming success and some great suggestions from readers, the author has completely revised the cookbook, including a new easy to read recipe format, correcting typographical errors, many new recipes, additional nutritional information and so on.

More than 50 new recipes have been added including a section of Vegetarian Main Dishes (for those times when you are entertaining your ovo-lacto vegetarian friends). Some of these new recipes came from the suggestions of readers of the first edition - thank you for your input.

Each recipe now includes a per serving analysis of calories, fat and protein, in addition to the grams of carbohydrates. Although this supplementary nutritional information is not necessary for those on the Dr. Atkins' Diet, it could be useful for those on the many other variations of a low-carb diet. The calculations for the nutritional analysis was based on United States Department of Agriculture (USDA) publications with some additional information obtained from food manufacturers. Not all sources agree, especially for the carbohydrates, which are often rounded off to the nearest whole gram. Therefore, the nutritional information shown on the recipes may vary slightly from other sources you may have.

The "Helpful Hints" section has been expanded, responding to frequently asked questions to the author from dieters new to the low-carb program. A section on Menu Planning & Shopping List has also been added.

If you have any comments, suggestions or feedback you would like to provide to the author for future editions, feel free to write her at the following address:

Lauri Ann Randolph
c/o Avalon Enterprises, Inc.
P.O. Box 1044
Golden, CO 80402-1044

TABLE OF CONTENTS

INTRODUCTION

You can lose 5 to 20 pounds per month on a low carbohydrate diet, easily, without hunger and enjoying each meal! I know that this is true because I did it; I lost 45 pounds in 5 months! That's almost 10 pounds per month, yet, I am metabolically resistive (more about that later). But if you are a typical overweight person, then you should be able to do better than me. My friend Suzan, who introduced me to the Dr. Atkins' Diet, lost 85 pounds in 6 months (and she even cheated from time to time)!

Contrary to popular belief, eating fatty foods does <u>not</u> make you fat. Also, eating a low-fat, high carbohydrate diet will <u>not</u> make you gain weight. But eating fatty foods <u>and</u> a lot of carbohydrates will make you fatter than the barn in no time!

So the wisdom of today, is that if you want to lose weight <u>without being hungry</u> then either go on a low-fat diet and don't worry about the carbohydrates or go on a low carbohydrate diet and don't worry about the fat. Well, I've tried both (and every other diet out there!) and the only one that has worked for me is the low carbohydrate diet.

But why? Well, for one thing, the foods I prefer to eat are fatty foods like, creamy sauces, a juicy steak, fried eggs & bacon, lots of real butter on my steamed vegetables, chocolate mousse. Sure, I like potatoes, pasta, bread and rice but they are just not satisfying to me without the sour cream, pesto sauce, butter and cheese I would prefer to put on top of them.

In order to have success with any diet, you must enjoy the foods that you are eating. If you feel that you can not survive without potatoes, pasta, bread, rice and sugar, then I suggest that you try a low-fat diet. However, I felt that way too at first, but what I found was that my desire for high carb foods diminished to almost nothing after the first week or so of eating a low-carb diet. It's worth a try.

Another reason the low carbohydrate diet has worked for me, is how I feel while dieting. When I indulge in high carbohydrate foods, I feel tired and lazy, so I feel that I need a lot of sugar and caffeine to keep me going. But on a low carbohydrate diet I have more energy than ever, which feels great; and that in turn increases my productivity in work and play which makes me feel even better!

But what about cholesterol? Well, I don't claim to be an expert as to why it works but my cholesterol level went down on the diet. Yes, from about 212 to 185 in 5 months! But better than that, the ratio of the LDL and HDL was much improved. For a better understanding, I recommend that you read *Dr. Atkins' New Diet Revolution*. Other sources regarding the low-carb diet are the books on the Protein Power Diet, the Sugar Buster Diet and the Carbohydrate Addicts' Diet. All of these books have some great information as to why the diet works.

So how low is low when you are talking about carbohydrates? Well, that depends primarily on your metabolism. As I mentioned earlier, I'm metabolically resistive. I have a hypothyroid condition and I am post-menopausal. So in order for me to lose weight I need to keep my carbs down to 12 - 15 grams per day (it's easier than you would think). But most people who have a normal metabolism can eat up to 25 grams or even 40 grams per day and still lose 10 - 15 pounds per month. The amount will be different for every one. If you are metabolically resistive it may take some time to find your limit. To learn more about this, please read *Dr. Atkins' New Diet Revolution*.

The diet is easy, but the first two weeks may be a challenge. This is because you will be going through withdrawals, especially if you normally eat a fair amount of sugar. I felt awful the first week and wasn't sure I could stick it out. But with the encouragement of a friend I made it past the induction period and then started to feel better than I had in years. Thank you Suzan!

The purpose of this book is not to explain how or why a low carbohydrate diet works but to give you some delicious recipes for whichever low-carb diet you choose. With variety in your diet, it will be easier to stay on the diet and lose all the weight you wish to lose.

There are not many low-carb cookbooks available on the market today (although I'm sure that more will become available with time). I suggest that you get several low-carb cookbooks and find as many recipes as you can that suit your tastes and style of cooking. I hope that you can find in this cookbook at least several dozen recipes you like enough to add to your normal menu. Variety is the spice of life!

Each recipe in this cookbook is less than 10 grams of carbohydrates per serving. But be careful about serving sizes and the number of servings you have. When I'm shedding pounds, I prefer to stay under 3g carbs per serving with an occasional splurge. If I'm in maintenance mode, then 6g per meal works fine for me.

Good Luck and happy cooking!

HELPFUL HINTS

There are a number of factors that can help you stay on the diet and lose weight fast. I have found these out through reading other materials and from my own personal experience.

Drink plenty of water. Water is crucial to the diet. The more you drink the more you lose! It's that simple. But beware, we are talking about water, not sodas, coffee or tea. Just plain water. You can add a slice of lemon, but you are adding 1 - 3 grams of carbohydrates. You can also add a drop of lemon or orange extract for less than 1 gram. Pure, filtered water is the best. If your tap water does not taste good to you, then purchase a water filter or buy bottled water.

Don't get too hungry. When you let yourself get very hungry, you are more likely to make bad choices in what to eat, especially if you are away from home. I keep individually wrapped string cheese with me where ever I go. It can go days without refrigeration and it can get me through most temptations. As soon as you realize you are hungry, drink as much water as possible to slow the hunger. Then go eat foods that are on the diet.

Have the right foods available at all times. Stock your refrigerator and pantry with plenty of foods you can eat. I have found that having pre-prepared foods available at all times, helps ever so much. I almost always have the following items on hand:

- Breakfast squares (there are many recipes included in this cookbook). Breakfast squares not only make breakfast easier, they are great snacks too.

- Hard boiled eggs. Deviled eggs fall into this category too.

- An assortment of cheeses.

- A pot of soup. Most soups get better after a day or two so I always make enough for at least three days.

- Pork rinds. If you don't already like them, you may soon develop a taste for them, basically because they are so very crunchy. I don't care for them plain, but I have several dips for them.

- Macadamia nuts. These are the lowest in carbs (3.8g carbs/oz). Brazil nuts and pine nuts are about 4.0g carbs per ounce. Sesame seeds and sunflower seeds are 5.3g per ounce. If you are not metabolically resistive then there are other nuts you can have in small quantities too (most are 6 to 8g carbs/oz).

- Sugar free Jell-O. I like it best with a few tablespoons of cream poured on top. It's not only a good dessert but a great snack too, especially when the sugar cravings start.

- Sweet'n Low hard candies. These are about 3g carbs each, but can get me through a sugar craving better than soda or Jell-O.

- Green olives stuffed with pimento. These have only 1g of carbs for about 4 olives. Sometimes I just stare at the open refrigerator, not really hungry but just want a little something to eat. I reach for the olives.

You will find your own favorites, but until you do, try the above items. The key is to have plenty of the right foods available, so it is easier to make the right choice.

Have quick and easy meals always on hand. Many of the recipes in this book are quick and easy, but others take some time for preparation. For me, it's a lot easier to drive past Taco Bell at dinner time, if I know that once I get home it will be only a matter of minutes before I can sit down to delicious food. So when you take the time to prepare something, make extra servings. Many of the recipes can be frozen and then reheated in a microwave a week or two later. That way you are not eating the same thing day after day. Just put each extra servings in separate freezer bags or Tupperware and you have a meal ready in no time. [Caution: most egg dishes do not freeze well].

Going Out to Eat: Most restaurants have many things on the menu that you should be able to eat and still stay on the diet. In general, the exceptions are Chinese, Italian and pizza places; these are the most challenging and probably should be avoided. Mexican restaurants are limiting also. I usually order fajitas without the tortillas and ask that chips not be brought to the table.

Most restaurants have several meat, chicken and fish entree selections, just be sure that they are not breaded. Many places are happy to provide substitutions and variations so don't be afraid to ask. Try to avoid having things brought to the table that you know you should stay away from, like dinner rolls. If it's not on your plate, you won't be as tempted to eat the things you should avoid.

Remember to ask for no croutons on your salad and order blue cheese, Caesar, oil & vinegar or ranch dressing - these are always safe choices. "House dressings" often have some sugar or other "to be avoided" ingredients; as does most Italian, Thousand Island and fruit vinaigrettes.

Request a substitution for potatoes of any kind. Perhaps they will have sautéed mushrooms, tomato slices, cottage cheese, creamed spinach, steamed broccoli or other acceptable vegetable.

Sometimes for lunch, I'll order a cheese burger without the bun and substitute vegetables for the fries. Remember to ask about the details of the vegetable of the day, if it is carrots, peas, corn, etc. then get a salad w/o croutons. Also, avoid getting cole slaw since it is usually made with sugar.

Fast Foods: Just stay away from them if you can. But if in a pinch go to Boston Market or similar chicken drive-thru.

At Kentucky Fried Chicken, Boston Market and the like, order the rotisserie chicken (not all locations have it) or just pull the breading off the original recipe chicken. Remember to state "no sides or bread" so that you are not tempted.

Hamburger joints are disastrous for me. But some people have the discipline to remove the bread and just eat the meat and cheese. I find this easier at Arby's just picking out the roast beef and dabbing it with "horsey sauce".

Taco Bell had always been my favorite fast food place! But their menu is so very limited if you really want to stay with the diet. Now, when tempted, I order the "big beef burrito supreme" (be sure to state "no beans" since each location seems to make it differently). I then unwrap it and eat the insides with a fork (please don't try this while driving!!) and discard the tortilla.

Zero Carbohydrate Foods: The only foods that do not have any carbohydrates are fresh meats, poultry and most fish. You can have as much as you want of these foods. Eggs (0.3g carbs each) and most shellfish are very low in carbs, but not zero, so be careful.

Many other foods are very low in carbohydrates, but that does not mean that you can have as much as you want and still lose weight. You must use moderation and always read the labels carefully. I recommend that you purchase a small book of carbohydrate gram counter and use it often. Count every gram you eat for at least 1 month so that you become accustomed to the amount of carbs in the foods you prefer.

Some foods may show 0g carbs per serving on the label (e.g., some cheeses, dill pickles, olives, pre-packaged meats products, diet sodas, etc.), but **don't believe it**. Label makers are allowed to say 0g carbohydrates if the serving size has less than 1.0 grams. This means if a serving size has 0.9g carbs, then they are allowed to print 0g carbs on the label. Just to make it easier on yourself, you should assume that unless it is fresh meat or poultry then the recommended serving has 1.0g carbs. This will help keep you from overindulging. Watch out for diet soda at ~ 0.5g carbs per can.

Do not assume that if a food is high in protein that it is also low in carbs. For example: 1 cup of kidney beans has 43g protein (which is high) but it also has over 110g of carbs (which will blow your diet for many, many days if not weeks).

The Onion Family: The different types of onions have different amounts of carbs. So choose wisely. For the first two weeks on the diet it might be best to avoid onions completely and use only onion salt, scallions (green onions), chives and garlic.

Item	Carbs	Item	Carbs
1 ave. yellow onion	8.6	1 clove of garlic	1.0
1 ave. white onion	12.7	1 ave. shallot	4.3
1 ave. red onion	13.8	1 Tbsp chives	0.2
1 ave. leek (whole)	17.5	1 scallion (whole)	2.5
1 ave. leek (white part only)	7.5	1 scallion (white part only)	1.0

Fruit: More than anything else, I miss fruit the most when I'm on this diet. After the first two weeks you can sneak a nibble here and there but be cautious - a little adds up fast. Stick with the first several items listed below and just have a little. I've listed the others just in case you are ever tempted to cheat. One banana and you have blown it!

½ cup of fruit	Carbs	½ cup of fruit	Carbs
rhubarb	2.8	oranges	10.6
grapefruit	4.7	tangerine	10.9
strawberries	5.2	lemon	12.3
watermelon	5.7	cherries	12.4
cantaloupe	6.7	pears	12.5
papaya	6.9	grapes	13.9
cranberries	7.0	mango	14.0
raspberries	7.1	kiwi fruit	15.1
apples	8.4	figs	19.0
peaches	9.4	plums	19.0
pineapple	9.6	banana	26.2
blueberries	10.1	raisins	57.4
lime	10.5	dates	65.1

Technically, rhubarb is not a fruit but I like it zapped in the microwave with a little Sweet'N Low and nutmeg. Then topped with cream. It's a great, tangy, low-carb dessert.

Pasta Sauces: Most of the white sauces (Alfredo, Four Cheese, Creamy Pesto) are quite low in carbs, but check the labels anyway. As for commercial red sauces, there are a lot of different kinds and most are made with sugar and are very high in carbs.

One exception that I have found is the Classico brand. These vary from 6 to 11grams carbs per ½ cup serving. I love their Tomato Alfredo Sauce. Use it over chicken, served with steamed vegetables tossed with butter, garlic and parmesan cheese - now you have a quick Italian dinner.

Going to the Movies: Resisting popcorn at the movies is not always easy. I sneak in a bag of nuts, some string cheese and Trident cinnamon gum. All this plus a large diet soda and I'm satisfied.

Sweeteners: I use Sweet'N Low almost exclusively. Stevia is a natural product but tastes quite strange to me. NutraSweet and Equal loses it's sweetening power if heated (and when heated, they are reported to break down into toxic by-products - very scary!). For the dessert recipes that do not require heating, feel free to substitute NutraSweet or Equal. Mixing different types of sweeteners together has the most sweetening effect.

Alcohol: Even though there is wine & sherry in several recipes, theses are not zero carb items. Pure liquors have no carbs - but typical mixed drinks are loaded. I prefer the taste of sherry, but you can substitute red or white wine for any of the recipes for a slightly lower carb count.

1 oz Liquor	Carbs	1 oz Liquor	Carbs
sherry	2.3g	vodka	0.0g
red wine	0.5g	scotch	0.0g
white wine	0.2g	gin	0.0g
vermouth	1.6g	bourbon	0.0g
beer	2.1g	brandy	0.0g
Grand Marnier	10.4g	whiskey	0.0g
Amaretto	8.5g	tequila	0.0g
Kahlua	13.6g	rum	0.0g

Popsicles: Popsicles now has a sugar free option. They are only 3g carbs each and are a wonderful summertime dessert.

Gum: I have found that Trident gum is the lowest in carbs at 1g per stick. Their cinnamon gum helps me get through a movie without popcorn..

Breathe Mints: Most "breathe mints" are loaded with sugar, so be aware. I like the Tic Tac brand, especially the orange and cinnamon. These have just under 1g carb for a serving of 2.

Vitamins. Taking the right vitamins will keep cravings for certain foods to a minimum. If you do nothing else take a one-a-day multivitamin with minerals. I think taking extra vitamin C is a good idea since the diet is so low on vitamin C rich foods. However, I recommend that you read Dr. Atkins' book for more suggestions.

Estrogen: If you are taking any estrogen ·product for hormone replacement therapy or birth control, you will probably be metabolically resistive. So try to keep your total carb count below 15- 20g per day.

Thermogenic herbs. There are a number of thermogenic herbs and other fat burners on the market that are available almost anywhere vitamins are sold. Many of them work quite well, others don't seem to do a thing. The ones I prefer are from Herbal Life (not sold in stores). Once I started taking the "green and tan" twice daily, the weight loss was faster. They also had the benefit of curbing my appetite and boosting my energy.

Ketosis sticks. These are strips of treated paper that you dip in your urine to indicate the level of fat burning that is happening. Read Dr. Atkins' book for a full explanation. The primary benefit is that during those frustrating plateaus in your weight loss program (and there will be many; it's a natural phenomenon) the ketosis sticks let you know that you are burning fat even though the scale might not reflect this fact.

Exercise. Any form or type of exercise is helpful in any weight loss program. I prefer swimming, but those that increase your body temperature work better, such as walking, jogging, tread mill, dancing and most other aerobic endeavors. Just start off slow and be patient with yourself. Ideally, you'll want to do at least 45 minutes 3 to 4 days per week.

If you have reached a weight loss plateau and you are being very careful with your carbohydrate intake, then step up your exercise program for a while. Usually adding just 15 minutes more for two or three days in a row can break the plateau.

Alpine Bakery. I have discovered a great bakery that will ship food items to you ($35 minimum order). They specialize in low carbohydrate treats, such as breads, cookies, eclairs, muffins, cheese cake, pudding, etc. I am particularly partial to their chocolate eclairs and chocolate cookies.

Since their products do not use wheat flour, the texture of the bread-like items are a bit strange and spongy. But they are delicious once you become accustomed to their texture. The exception is the flat bread which reminds be of pita bread in texture. Toasting their flat bread is quite useful for dips and things you would expect to eat with crackers. The cinnamon-raison flat bread is also great for a quick breakfast. These items will be particularly helpful if you are addicted to breads.

Their pancake mix makes great blintzes, and of course pancakes. The mix is also good for a type of smoothie . I blend it with cream, ice and ½ teaspoon of orange extract. You could add a strawberry or two, also.

Alpine Bakery Inc.
686 NE 33rd Street
Pompano Beach, FL 33064
(954) 942-7560 or 1-800-940-7560

Webpage: Alpine Bakery.com/specialty

Dr. Atkins Products. There are a number of low carb foods offered through The Atkins Center. They also offer nutritional supplements, vacation cruises, and a newsletter. Contact the center for a complete catalog.

The Atkins Center for Complementary Medicine
152 East 55th Street
New York, NY 10022
1-888- DR ATKINS
(888) 372-8546
Website: www.atkinscenter.com

Reward Yourself. It is extremely important to acknowledge your progress and successes. Hopefully you have a friend that can give you support and acknowledgment along the way. But also, you should give yourself a <u>non-food</u> treat for every 5 or 10 pounds that you lose. This may seem silly but it can really help stimulate your motivation. Reward yourself with a new CD, book, video, sweater, a manicure, a massage, flowers, tools or accessories for your favorite hobby, a plant, computer software, a nice decorative candle or any other "unnecessary" item.

Your reward does not have to cost money, however. Give yourself some time off from your busy schedule to lay in the park and watch the clouds roll by, take a long drive in the country, visit a local art gallery or museum, take a walk and collect wild flowers (not your neighbors!) or interesting dried weeds, volunteer to be an usher at a play you've been wanting to see, go dancing with your significant other, visit a local historical site, or any other engaging activity that is not part of your normal routine.

Once you have reached your desired weight - CELEBRATE! You deserve the very best that you can afford for accomplishing a very important goal. Plan this event early in your weight loss program and start saving for it. This can be absolutely anything, as long as it is special to you. Throw yourself a party, take a vacation, go on a Dr. Atkins vacation cruise, buy a new wardrobe, get a new computer, take that art or music class you've been dreaming about, enjoy a weekend at a quaint bed & breakfast, learn to fly or scuba dive, have a room in your house redecorated, buy a new car, get supplies to start a new hobby, or perhaps take a hot air balloon ride. Give this some conscious thought and let your imagination soar. Achieving your desired weight is a major achievement and deserves celebration. Congratulations!

Take care of your emotional self. Last but not least, it is imperative that you address your food issue(s). For most over weight people, there is an underlying emotional cause for over indulging in food. Perhaps it is depression, anger, lack of self confidence, exhaustion, a stressful relationship, boredom or a variety of serious issues. Food is often used as a form of comfort, self protection, self nurturing, or simply to numb certain feelings. Food can be a serious addiction. If you are over weight, it is highly likely that you "use" food to mask some issue(s) which you would rather not face directly.

There are many ways to identify and get support for your underlying issue(s). Spiritual counseling, therapy and support groups (e.g., Overeaters Anonymous) are certainly one approach. But there are also a multitude of self-help books. Understanding why you over-use food is the first step to changing the behavior.

I truly believe the primary reason that diets don't work for most people is that they are addressing the symptom and not the cause(s) of the problem(s). Many people are stuffing their feelings by stuffing their face. This is generally an unconscious behavior and therefore can be difficult to self-diagnose. Your overeating patterns and behavior is probably a complex phenomenon and deserves considerable attention. Be gentle, patient, self-compassionate and don't over criticize yourself. But be ruthless in coming to an understanding of your particular relationship with food. The goal is not necessarily to eliminate your issues, but to conquer their controlling influence over the way you make food choices.

When I get triggered and really want a particular food that I should not have, I need to voice it <u>out loud</u> in order to truly release it. For example, I get triggered for mashed potatoes from time to time. When I let myself have them, I blow my diet for days and I feel so guilty. But what is worse, is that they usually don't even taste that good (since I've lost my taste for most high-carb foods) nor do they provide the comfort I was seeking. So now I say <u>out loud</u>, with the full force of emotion that I'm feeling at the time, "I want mashed potatoes". Then I say with as much conviction as I can drum up, "But I choose not to have it." If the craving doesn't go away in a minute or two then I make "mock mashed potatoes" as soon as I get a chance (see recipe inside) and take a deep look at what is really going on inside of my heart or head that I am craving something that is self-destructive to me. Is it just that others were having it and stating how good it is; am I feeling tired, sad, or blue; how am I feeling uncomfortable; is my self-esteem being challenged in some way; is some fear showing up that way; why am I not feeling self-loving; … ? I keep asking myself questions until I find what is triggering a desire for something that does not support me. Then I try to deal with <u>that</u> issue instead of eating mashed potatoes. It can be hard work, but like all things, with practice it gets so much easier.

I believe that when one starts to lose weight, not only are the fat deposits released, but also the toxins and emotions which were stuffed in there while overeating. As you lose weight, you may notice old feelings and memories coming up and then you may want to react in your old, familiar, comforting way, by overeating or indulging in a specific type of food. With conscious help and support, you should be able to resist, but it's good to know there are many zero and low carb foods to help you, if you simply must have a binge.

There seems to be a "last in, first out" relationship. So the more weight you lose the more you will reach into the past. This can cause some emotional and physical discomfort which you might not initially recognize nor understand. This can cause additional stress and can easily trigger the desire for the comfort foods you were using then. Older issues and experiences are generally harder to address because they may have been forgotten. But as you lose the weight they will most likely resurface in some way. However, if you understand the general process, have good support and apply conscious effort, you can conquer any demon. Be sure to drink plenty of water to help flush out these toxins and emotions faster.

I wish you the best of luck on your diet! Enjoy your meals and take very good care of yourself!

MENU PLANNING

Planning ahead is always a good idea in any undertaking. If you are just starting a low-carb diet for the first time, then you will need to do a fair amount of planning until your new eating program becomes routine.

What you plan for each meal will depend entirely on the amount of time you have and where you will be eating each meal. If you have a stressful job and/or work long hours, then you will need to do a lot of planning so that you are less likely to "cheat". If you are fortunate enough to work at home or only have a part-time job then planning can be minimal.

Breakfast: Do you normally eat breakfast? If not, just skip it and plan on having a mid-morning snack instead. This may consist of some cheese or a few slices of turkey, ham, roast beef or maybe two deviled eggs or simply a hard-boiled egg.

Breakfast squares are a great idea for those of you on the run. Make a batch on your day off and then you already have breakfast ready for the rest of your work week. During the winter months you will most like want to heat-up a square in the microwave. But during the warmer months you can just eat them cold straight out of the refrigerator. There are several breakfast square recipes in this book, but be creative and make-up some of your own with mine as a guide.

Making bacon and eggs in the morning is not quite as fast, but pretty close. I cook the bacon in the microwave, wrapped in paper towel and zapped for about 4 minutes. Meanwhile, I fry up some eggs.

If you have traditionally eaten toast and jam for breakfast, I suggest that you purchase the raison cinnamon flat bread from Alpine Bakery. These toast rather well and you can use a small amount of the sugar free jams or cream cheese on top. This is a good approach if your family is eating cereal for breakfast and that is triggering a desire for carbs.

On your days off you can be more creative with breakfast. Try the "hash browns" or "mock potato pancake" if you have a little time. For a Sunday brunch you might try the sweet omelet rolls, egg foo young or eggs Florentine.

Lunch: Again, depending where you normally eat lunch, this may take some planning. If you are at home, this is not a problem. There are so many choices, including a variety of soups and salads.

If you take your lunch to work, then you'll probably need to prepare something the night before and put it in Tupperware or the like. Again soups and salads are always a good idea. But you'll need access to a microwave for the soup. There are a lot of different soup and salad choices in this cookbook. I suggest also having a stash of cheese at work. If you don't have a refrigerator available at work then try the individually wrapped string cheese. These do not need refrigeration for days, but don't leave them in a sunny spot either.

If you normally go out for lunch, this takes a little planning too. The primary plan is not to let yourself get too hungry before you go out, otherwise you may be tempted to cheat. It is best to eat at the same time everyday. Your body will get use to the schedule quickly and save you from temptations. I suggest drinking a large glass of water before leaving for lunch, this will slow your appetite so that you can make better choices. Again, having a stash of cheese available is highly recommended, since there will be times when you just can't get away at your normal time.

Dinner: This meal does not have to be a problem to plan. I usually think of the various types of dinners I think I'd like that week and go shopping for them all at once. Then when dinner time rolls around, I just decide then what I want specifically that day.

It's a good idea, to make extra servings when you cook dinner. This way you can either freeze a portion for next week or have basically the same thing two days in a row. Most meats and poultry have a few variations that can be employed for the following day. For example, if I'm going to grill a steak for dinner then I often grill two and put one in the refrigerator.

The following day, I might sauté some scallions and mushrooms then throw in the cut up steak - there's dinner. Grilled chicken is just as easy. Have plain grilled chicken one night and then use the left-over portion with a sauce or cheese the next day.

If your family is not on the diet with you, then you will have a bit of a challenge, but you need not make two completely different dinners. Your goal will be to satisfy their tastes without putting yourself in a place of wanting their food. The primary approach to this, is to be sure that your meal is not too very much different from theirs. The temptations are usually triggered from a smell or visual input rather than a true craving.

Generally, every one in the family can eat your main course and salad (although you must skip out on the croutons and choose a low carb dressing). Side vegetables may need to be different in some cases but make them similar is color and texture. For example, if you are serving your family mashed potatoes with a meat, then fix yourself the "mock mashed potatoes" made with cauliflower. If your family wants peas and carrots, then fix yourself steamed broccoli (cut small) with bits of red bell pepper thrown in.

If your family is having pasta or pizza then fix yourself one of the "spaghetti" recipes in this book matching the color and smell of their sauce. Spaghetti squash with a cheese sauce is a great substitute for their macaroni & cheese.

Dessert: If you normally have a sweet-tooth then planning dessert is a must. Check out the dessert section and <u>plan</u> a dessert for each night. The Jell-O recipes are good for several nights.

<u>Variety is good</u>. Try not to make the same 3 meals over and over again. If you get bored with your food, you will be tempted to cheat. Use your days off to go through this cookbook, come up with your meal plans, then immediately go shopping.

SHOPPING LIST

If you are just getting started on Dr. Atkins' diet then you will need to go through the induction period and will mostly just purchase meats, poultry, fish, eggs, cheese and some lettuce. Please read his book for the specifics.

After completing the two week induction period, and your cupboards are bare (or just have high carb foods) then start off with the following list. This list assumes cooking for 1 for a week. This list may look overwhelming but many items you may already have and some items will carry over to following weeks, such as the condiments.

- Meat, poultry and fish for dinners. Get 7 portions or more (you can always freeze left-overs). I suggest:
    - 2 steaks, any type
    - 2 servings of pork chops, spare ribs or a pork loin
    - 2 servings chicken, Cornish game hens or a whole roasted chicken
    - 1 serving fish or seafood (eat the fish the first day, since it doesn't keep long, unless frozen)
- 1 lb sliced meats - turkey, roast beef and/or ham. These are great for lunches and snacks. But watch out for pre-packaged meats, they usually have sugar added.
- 2 - 4 cans of tuna
- 2 dozen eggs - this will be enough for making a batch of breakfast squares, some hard boil eggs for snacks and some left over for fried eggs and other dishes.
- 1 lb bacon
- 2 lbs of assorted cheeses.
- 8 to 16 ounces of cream cheese
- 3 or 4 pints heavy whipping cream

- Assorted vegetables. Get some of them frozen, because there is more than a week's worth here. I suggest:
  - 1 head broccoli, or 1 bag frozen broccoli
  - 1 head cauliflower, or 1 bag frozen cauliflower
  - 1 head of cabbage
  - 1 serving of zucchini or yellow squash
  - 1 bunch spinach, or frozen chopped spinach
  - 1 or two green bell peppers
  - 1 bunch scallions (green onion)
  - 1 yellow onion
  - 1 or 2 cucumbers
  - 1 or 2 tomatoes
  - 1 head of lettuce
  - ½ lb of mushroom (or get canned mushrooms)
  - celery
  - 1 bunch of cilantro
  - 1 bunch of parsley
  - 1 or 2 bulbs of garlic
  - 1 stalk fresh ginger
- A few ribs of rhubarb or 4 - 6 strawberries
- 2 lemons or limes
- 1 jar Classico Tomato Alfredo sauce
- 1 jar white pasta sauce
- 1 jar salsa (check labels!)
- 1 package commercial pesto sauce
- 1 can green chilies, chopped
- 1 jar green olives
- 1 can black olives
- 1 can artichoke hearts
- 2 cans chicken broth
- 1 jar mayonnaise
- 1 jar mustard
- 1 jar olive oil

- 1 jar vinegar
- 1 jar soy sauce
- 1 jar cooking wine or sherry
- 1 jar Kitchen Bouquet
- 1 jar Nellie & Joe's Key West lime juice
- 1 jar Mrs. Dash salt substitute (I like the garlic blend)
- 2 boxes sugar free Jell-O
- 1 box Sweet'N Low (packets or bulk)
- 1 jar sugar-free jelly
- 1 jar chunky peanut butter
- diet soda (my favorites are, Diet Dr. Pepper, Pepsi One, Fresca and diet root beer)
- 1 bag pork rinds
- 1 jar macadamia nut
- ½ lb other nuts, such as cashews

Yes, this list looks quite overwhelming and yes it will cost a bundle, but it's the best way to get started.

Meats are expensive so I usually buy a lot of whatever is on sale and put some in the freezer. Many meats and poultry come already frozen, such as chicken (including buffalo wings), Cornish game hens, turkey, hamburger patties, etc. Be careful of pre-packaged frozen fish, they are usually breaded.

As always, be sure to read every label carefully. Also compare brands, you might be amazed at the variations in carbohydrates of the "same" food item.

Breakfast

BREAKFAST

Cream Cheese & Tomato Omelet
Custard Breakfast Squares
Egg Foo Yung
Eggs Benedict
Eggs Florentine
Eggs Merritt House
Florentine Omelet Breakfast Squares
Hash Browns
Huevos Rancheros
Mock Potato Pancakes
Onion-Cheese Frittata
Saturday Morning Scramble
Southwestern Breakfast Squares
Sweet Breakfast Rolls
Swiss Eggs
Western Omelet Breakfast Squares

Cream Cheese & Tomato Omelet

6 eggs
¼ cup cream
    salt & pepper, to taste
¼ cup butter
6 oz cream cheese, cubed
1 whole tomato, peeled, seeded & chopped

Makes 4 Servings	
Analysis per Serving:	
Carbs	**4.0g**
Calories	403.4
Fat	37.5g
Protein	13.3g

1. Beat eggs until light, then beat in cream, salt and pepper.

2. Melt butter in a large skillet. Pour eggs into skillet. When set, but still soft, spread tomatoes and cheese over top. Fold in half. When bottom is brown, flip over and brown other side.

Custard Breakfast Squares

10 eggs
1 pint heavy cream
1 pint water
1 tsp almond extract
5 packets Sweet'N Low®
1 tsp cinnamon

Makes 6 Servings	
Analysis per Serving:	
Carbs	**4.3g**
Calories	403.1
Fat	37.7g
Protein	12.1g

Set oven to 350°F

1. Beat the eggs. Add all ingredient except the cinnamon. Blend well.

2. Pour mixture into 8x8 non-metallic baking dish. Sprinkle cinnamon on top.

3. Place baking dish inside a larger baking dish of cool water. (The water should be at least ½ way up main baking dish. This is what makes the creamy texture.) Bake for 40 minutes. Let cool. Cut into 6 pieces. Refrigerate.

Serve cold or reheat serving in microwave for 1- 2 minutes.

Make this dish a day in advance. It also makes a great dessert.

Egg Foo Yung

1 cup bean sprouts (mung beans)
1 Tbsp butter
1/8 tsp ginger, fresh grated
    dash onion salt
4 eggs
2 Tbsp heavy cream
2 tsp soy sauce

Makes 2 Servings	
Analysis per Serving:	
Carbs	**5.3g**
Calories	269.6
Fat	21.3g
Protein	14.8g

1. Sauté bean sprouts in butter, ginger and onion salt until sprouts are translucent. Remove from skillet.

2. Beat eggs with cream. Mix in the bean sprouts.

3. Ladle 1/4 of mixture into skillet. Push eggs to form a patty. Once set, turn and brown. Remove from skillet, set aside and Repeat.

4. Drizzle each with soy sauce and serve.

Wasabi can be added to the soy sauce for an added zing.

Eggs Benedict

4 eggs, poached
4 slices Canadian bacon, cooked
4 slices tomato
½ cup hollandaise sauce
¼ tsp paprika

Makes 2 Servings	
Analysis per Serving:	
Carbs	**9.4g**
Calories	352.0
Fat	20.0g
Protein	27.6g

1. Poach Eggs: If you do not have an egg poacher than try this. Fill a large, deep skillet with 1 inch of water. Add 2 Tbsp white vinegar (helps hold the egg together) and a dash of salt (helps keeps the eggs from tasting like vinegar). Bring water to a simmer (do not boil). Carefully break eggs into water, cook until whites are firm. Remove with a slotted spoon. Serve immediately.

2. Place slices of tomato on top of each slice of Canadian bacon. Place poached eggs on top and pour the Hollandaise sauce over the eggs. Sprinkle with paprika. Serve immediately.

Eggs Florentine

4 eggs poached
4 slices tomato
1 cup spinach, cooked
½ cup hollandaise sauce
¼ tsp nutmeg

Makes 2 Servings	
Analysis per Serving:	
Carbs	**9.4g**
Calories	270.5
Fat	16.2g
Protein	16.7g

1. Poach Eggs: If you do not have an egg poacher than try this. Fill large, deep skillet with 1 inch of water. Add 2 Tbsp white vinegar and a dash of salt. Bring water to a simmer (do not boil). Carefully break eggs into water, cook until whites are firm. Remove with a slotted spoon. Serve immediately.

2. Place two slices of tomato on a plate. Heap ½ of the spinach over the tomato; place two poached eggs on top and pour ½ of the Hollandaise sauce over the eggs. Sprinkle with nutmeg. Repeat. Serve immediately.

Eggs Merritt House

4 eggs
2 oz ham, very thinly sliced
4 Tbsp cream
2 oz cheddar cheese, grated

Makes 2 Servings	
Analysis per Serving:	
Carbs	**3.5g**
Calories	387.5
Fat	29.9g
Protein	25.3g

Set oven to 450°F

1. Grease with oil, 2 boat shaped individual casserole dishes.

2. Crack 2 eggs into each dish. Pour 1 tablespoon of cream on one side of dish and 1 tablespoon on the other. Repeat for second dish.

3. Place the very thinly sliced ham over the eggs, covering the yolks. Sprinkle the cheese on top.

4. Cook in pre-heated oven for 10 minutes. Remove and serve immediately.

Notes:
1. This recipe comes from a wonderful and beautiful Bed & Breakfast Inn a few blocks from downtown Denver, CO called The Merritt House (303) 861-5230 or toll free 877-861-5230, http://merritthouse.com. One of their chefs is on the Dr. Atkins' diet!
2. Try using Swiss cheese and/or sliced turkey as variations.
3. This is a great way to serve a lot of people all at once, especially for those holiday times when you have many family and friends staying over.

Florentine Omelet Breakfast Squares

10 eggs
¼ cup heavy cream
1 bunch spinach, chopped
1 clove garlic crushed
1 Tbsp olive oil
2 Tbsp water
4 oz mushroom canned, sliced
2 Tbsp green onion, chopped
8 oz cream cheese
4 oz Romano cheese, grated
¼ tsp salt & pepper, each
¼ tsp nutmeg
¼ tsp paprika

Makes 8 Servings	
Analysis per Serving:	
Carbs	**7.4g**
Calories	466.1
Fat	35.8g
Protein	29.0g

Set oven to 350°F.

1. Lightly sauté garlic in olive oil on medium heat. Add water and spinach, cover. Let steam for 1 minute. Drain on paper towels.

2. Beat the eggs and cream. Mix other ingredient except cheeses and paprika, blend well.

3. Using a lightly greased (olive oil is best) 8 x 8 non-metallic baking dish, spread ½ of the spinach mixture on bottom. Cover the mixture with cream cheese (use your hands to make flatten pieces and place over spinach). Spread out remaining spinach mixture over cream cheese. Pour egg mixture over spinach. Sprinkle Romano cheese on top.

4. Bake for 40 minutes. Cut into 8 pieces. Serve at once. Refrigerate left over.

Hash Browns

1/2 head cauliflower, fresh & chopped
¼ green bell pepper, minced
1 Tbsp onion, minced
1 Tbsp butter
1 tsp cooking oil

Makes 2 Servings	
Analysis per Serving:	
Carbs	**2.3g**
Calories	80.9
Fat	8.0g
Protein	0.7g

Be sure that the vegetables are dry prior to cooking.

In a heavy skillet, melt butter on medium/high heat. Add remaining ingredient before butter starts to burn. Stir well to coat vegetables. Cook for 6 to 8 minutes (do not cover). Stir frequently but allow vegetables to brown. Serve hot.

Serve with eggs and bacon for no additional carbs.

Note: Do not try this with frozen cauliflower. It will just turn to mush. If you only have frozen cauliflower on hand then see "Mock Potato Pancakes".

Huevos Rancheros

3 Tbsp butter
2 Tbsp onion, finely chopped
1 clove garlic, minced
2 Tbsp green bell pepper, finely chopped
6 eggs
2 Tbsp mild salsa
2 oz Monterey jack cheese, shredded

Makes 4 Servings	
Analysis per Serving:	
Carbs	**3.2g**
Calories	438.9
Fat	33.4g
Protein	25.2g

1. Melt butter in large frying pan. Sauté onions, garlic, and pepper until soft.

2. Beat eggs until light and pour into frying pan. Cook over very low heat, stirring constantly. When eggs begin to harden, add salsa, continuing to cook and stir until eggs are set.

3. Add cheese, stir, Serve immediately.

Mock Potato Pancakes

12 oz frozen cauliflower
1 scallion, finely minced
1 large egg, well beaten
   salt & pepper, to taste
1 butter
2 Tbsp sour cream

Makes 4 Servings	
Analysis per Serving:	
Carbs	**4.8g**
Calories	56.0
Fat	3.0g
Protein	3.6g

1. Defrost and partially cook cauliflower in microwave (about 2 or 3 minutes) until tender. Drain. Begin to mash cauliflower so that it partially forms a paste but leave some small chunks. This may take a little practice. You can also separate the cauliflower into two batches - one smashed well, the other chopped.

2. Mix into well beaten egg, the cauliflower, green onions, salt & pepper. Mix well.

3. In a skillet, melt the butter on medium/high heat. Ladle a small amount of the mixture into the hot skillet. With a spatula, push in the sides to form a circle. The pancake should be small enough for your spatula to fit under completely. If your skillet is large enough, do two or more at a time. Cook until brown, flip over very carefully and brown the other side. Repeat until all are cooked. These can be kept warm in an oven until the rest of breakfast is ready.

4. Serve with a small dab of sour cream on each pancake.

Notes:
1. This recipe will take some practice to flip the pancakes whole.
2. These are great with bacon and eggs.
3. As an alternate top with grated cheese instead of the sour cream.

Onion-Cheese Frittata

2 Tbsp olive oil
1 small onion, minced
1/2 cup Parmesan cheese
6 eggs
1/2 tsp oregano
1/8 tsp nutmeg
1/2 tsp salt
1/4 tsp black pepper

Makes 4 Servings	
Analysis per Serving:	
Carbs	**4.7g**
Calories	232.4
Fat	17.6g
Protein	14.0g

Set oven to 350°F.

1. Sauté onion in oil until golden. Stir beaten eggs and all other ingredients into the pan. Mix well.

2. Pour into a greased glass baking dish and bake for about 30 minutes, or until set and top is golden.

Saturday Morning Scramble

5 eggs
1/4 cup heavy cream
1 tsp Mrs. Dash, garlic blend
1 green onion, chopped
1/4 cup green bell pepper, chopped
1 tsp butter
1 oz cheddar cheese, grated
2 oz cream cheese

Makes 2 Servings	
Analysis per Serving:	
Carbs	**9.6g**
Calories	489.1
Fat	40.2g
Protein	23.4g

1. Beat eggs well. Add cream and seasonings and beat well again.

2. Heat butter in nonstick skillet on medium/high heat. Sauté green onions and bell peppers for 1 minute.

3. Add eggs to skillet. Stirring occasionally, cook until just before "set".

4. Sprinkle cheddar cheese over eggs, stir once. Add cream cheese in small little dabs. Stir once and serve.

Serve with as much bacon as you like.

Southwestern Breakfast Squares

10 eggs
1/4 cup heavy cream
4 oz canned green chilies, diced
2 Tbsp salsa
1/4 tsp salt
1/2 cup bell pepper, diced
1 Tbsp onion, diced
1/2 cup Monterey jack cheese, shredded
1/2 cup cheddar cheese, shredded

Makes 6 Servings	
Analysis per Serving:	
Carbs	9.8g
Calories	267.2
Fat	18.4g
Protein	17.0g

Set oven to 350°F

1. Beat the eggs and cream. Add all ingredient except ½ the cheese and blend well.

2. Pour mixture into 8 x 8 non-metallic baking dish. Sprinkle extra cheese on top. Bake for 40 minutes.

3. Cut into 6 pieces. Serve at once. Refrigerate left-overs.

Makes a great main dish too.

Sweet Breakfast Rolls

5 eggs
2 Tbsp Alpine Bakery pancake mix
   (see Helpful Hints)
2 Tbsp heavy cream
1 packet Sweet 'n Low®
1/2 tsp cinnamon
1/4 tsp vanilla extract

Makes 2 Servings	
Analysis per Serving:	
Carbs	**4.3g**
Calories	439.4
Fat	37.8g
Protein	20.2g

FILLING
4 oz cream cheese
1/4 tsp cinnamon
1 packet Sweet 'n Low®

1. Beat eggs with cream. Add pancake mix, sweetener, cinnamon and vanilla, beat again. Don't worry about the lumps.

2. Filling: soften cream cheese in microwave. Add cinnamon & sweetener and mix well.

3. Pour 1/4 of egg mixture into a buttered non-stick skillet on medium-high heat. Tip skillet so egg mixture covers bottom. Cook until solid and slightly browned, flip(ever so carefully) and cook until slightly browned. Remove to plate and repeat, making 4 thin omelets.

4. Spread 1/4 of cream cheese mixture over each omelet and roll up. Serve.

Swiss Eggs

1 Tbsp butter
1/4 lb Gruyere cheese, sliced thin
4 eggs
1/4 cup heavy cream
1 tsp salt
1/2 tsp black pepper
1/2 cup Parmesan cheese, grated

Makes 2 Servings	
Analysis per Serving:	
Carbs	**3.4g**
Calories	628.6
Fat	51.1g
Protein	38.5g

Set oven to 350°F

1. Pour melted butter into a shallow casserole dish.

2. Line dish with thin cheese slices.

3. Break the eggs neatly into the casserole dish, keeping them whole.

4. Add salt and pepper to cream, and carefully pour over the eggs.

5. Sprinkle with Parmesan cheese and bake at 350° for 10 minutes. Brown the cheese topping under the broiler for a few minutes, if necessary.

Western Omelet Breakfast Squares

10 eggs
1/4 cup heavy cream
  4 oz ham, cooked and diced
1/4 tsp salt
1/2 cup bell pepper, diced
  2 Tbsp onion, minced
  4 oz cheddar cheese, shredded

Makes 6 Servings	
Analysis per Serving:	
Carbs	9.5g
Calories	665.7
Fat	47.0g
Protein	46.6g

Set oven to 350°F

1. Beat the eggs and cream. Add all ingredient and blend well.

2. Pour mixture into 8 x 8 non-metallic baking dish. Sprinkle extra cheese on top if desired. Bake for 40 minutes.

3. Cut into 6 pieces. Serve at once. Refrigerate left over.

Appetizers and Snacks

APPETIZERS & SNACKS

Artichoke Heart Dip
Bacon & Onion Dip
Baked Artichoke Savories
Balsamic Onion and Cheese Picks
Blue Cheese & Brandy Spread
Buffalo Wings
Caviar & Deviled Eggs
Cheese "Crackers"
Cheese Balls
Chile Con Queso
Crab Dip
Cubed Ham with Horseradish Sauce
Grilled Sausage with Spicy Mustard
Guacamole
Marinated Mushrooms & Artichokes
Portabella Mushrooms with Brie & Pesto
Salmon Rolls
Salmon Stuffed Mushrooms
Salsa & Cream Cheese Dip
Sister Cream Cheese
Smoked Clam Dip
Spicy Deviled Eggs
Spinach Dip
Teriyaki Wings
Tomato & Mozzarella

Artichoke Heart Dip

1 can artichoke hearts, (10 oz)
1/2 cup mayonnaise
1/2 cup sour cream
1 cup Romano cheese, grated

Makes 6 Servings	
Analysis per Serving:	
Carbs	**3.1g**
Calories	251.6
Fat	24.6g
Protein	7.2g

Mix all ingredients well and pour into baking dish. Bake uncovered at 350F for 25 minutes. Serve with celery stick, bell pepper strips or pork rinds.

Bacon & Onion Dip

1 pint sour cream
2 scallions, chopped
2 Tbsp bacon bits
1/2 pkg Hidden Valley Ranch
    Bacon & Onion Dip Mix

Makes 8 Servings	
Analysis per Serving:	
Carbs	**3.2g**
Calories	131.4
Fat	12.4g
Protein	2.5g

1. Mix 1/2 to 2/3 of the dip mix into 1 pint of sour cream (Although the package says to use the entire contents per pint of sour cream, I find this flavor much too strong).

2. Add chopped scallions reserving a small portion as garnish. Serve dip in a flat bowl. Garnish with bacon bits and reserved chopped scallions.

Serve with pork rinds and celery sticks.

Baked Artichoke Savories

2 Tbsp chopped green onion
1 tsp pressed garlic
1 Tbsp dry sherry
1 Tbsp butter
3 egg whites
1 whole egg
2 Tbsp minced parsley
1/4 tsp dried dill
1/8 tsp cayenne pepper
1 cup grated mozzarella cheese
1/2 cup ricotta cheese
10 oz marinated artichoke hearts, drained and chopped

Makes 16 Servings	
Analysis per Serving:	
Carbs	**6.9g**
Calories	76.7
Fat	3.3g
Protein	5.9g

Set oven to 350°F.   Lightly oil an 8-inch square baking pan.

1. In a heavy skillet over medium-high heat, sauté onion and garlic in sherry and butter until soft but not browned.

2. Lightly beat egg whites until soft peaks form. Spoon into a bowl and mix with beaten whole egg, parsley, dill, cayenne, cheeses, and artichokes. Add sautéed onion and garlic. Pour into oiled baking pan.

3. Bake until set (about 30 minutes). Let cool, then cut into about 16 squares. Serve warm or cold.

Balsamic Onion and Cheese Picks

2 lb. pearl onions
1/3 cup olive oil
1/4 cup balsamic vinegar
   salt & pepper, to taste
3/4 lb Italian fontina cheese, cut into
    1/3-inch cubes
25 cocktail skewers

Makes 25 Servings	
Analysis per Serving:	
Carbs	**0.7g**
Calories	80.2
Fat	7.1g
Protein	3.5g

Set oven to 375°F

1. Blanch onions in boiling, salted water 30 seconds; drain. Slice off the root end. "Peel" the onions by pressing them slightly between your fingers; the inner part will slip out of the papery skin.

2. Whisk together oil, vinegar, salt, and pepper. Put onions in a roasting pan, add oil-vinegar mixture, and toss to coat well. Bake at 375°F until tender (about 25 minutes). Remove from oven and let cool in pan. Taste; adjust seasoning as necessary.

3. To serve, place 2 onions and 1 cheese cube on each cocktail skewer.

Blue Cheese & Brandy Spread

8 oz blue cheese, crumbled
16 oz cream cheese
1 cup brandy
3 Tbsp heavy cream
1 tsp thyme, powdered
   salt and pepper, to taste

Makes 8 Servings	
Analysis per Serving:	
Carbs	**6.8g**
Calories	974.6
Fat	85.4g
Protein	30.4g

Soften cream cheese. Mix well all ingredients. Let sit for 1 hour (2 hours if refrigerated) so flavors can meld. Serve stuffed in celery, mushroom or endive. Or wrap it in a thin slice of ham, turkey, roast beef or lettuce leaf. This is also great on toasted flat bread from the Alpine Bakery.

Buffalo Wings

24 chicken wings
1/2 cup oil
1/4 cup vinegar
  1 tsp Tabasco sauce
  1 tsp garlic salt
  1 cup blue cheese dressing
  4 celery ribs, cut into sticks

Makes 8 Servings	
Analysis per Serving:	
Carbs	**3.6g**
Calories	879.1
Fat	72.8g
Protein	51.1g

1. Mix oil, vinegar, Tabasco sauce and garlic powder. Marinate wings for at least one hour.

2. Bake wings at 400°F for 20 minutes. Pour off any liquids. Baste with marinate and broil until brown (5-10 minutes). Turn over, baste and broil again.

Serve with celery sticks and blue cheese dressing.

Caviar & Deviled Eggs

5 eggs
2 Tbsp sour cream
1 tsp onion, finely chopped
5 tsp caviar

Makes 5 Servings	
Analysis per Serving:	
Carbs	**5.2g**
Calories	312.2
Fat	27.1g
Protein	13.1g

1. Hard boil eggs (bring to a boil and then 8 -10 minutes on medium heat). Plunge into cold water. Let cool.

2. Peel eggs and slice long wise. Gently remove yolks and place in small bowl. Add sour cream to yolks and blend well. Add onions and blend well.

3. Spoon yolk mixture into hollow of eggs whites. Sprinkle each with ½ tsp of caviar. A small sprig of parsley makes a nice garnish too.

Cheese "Crackers"

8 oz Parmesan cheese		**Makes 10 Servings**	
1 Tbsp pancake mix		Analysis per Serving:	
(Dr. Atkins' or Alpine Bakery)		Carbs	0.9g
2 Tbsp water		Calories	103.4
vegetable oil		Fat	6.8g
		Protein	9.4g

1. Blend water and pancake mix to form a paste. Coarsely grate cheese (do not use the stuff in the green can). Mix cheese and paste together with hands. Add any spices you like such as cumin, garlic, chives or none at all. <u>Do not use salt</u>. Take about 1 tablespoon of mixture and form a patty in palm of hand. Form approx. 10 patties.

2. Place non-stick skillet on medium high heat, lightly coat with vegetable oil. Garlic flavored "PAM" spray works well. Place 3 to 5 of the patties in the skillet. Using a spatula push edges inward to shape. When slightly browned (about 1 minute) carefully flip each patty. Flatten with spatula. Brown again. <u>This technique requires some practice</u>. The darker brown, the more crispy the "cracker". Flip as many times as needed to desired color. For a crispier "cracker" eliminate the pancake mix and water.

3. Remove from skillet and place on paper towel to soak up excess oils.

4. Repeat until all patties are cooked. Serve as is or top them with a spread.

These "crackers" are quite salty but you can tone them down by serving with a mild spread such as cream cheese, a dab of Ranch dressing, or try guacamole.

Cheese Balls

5 oz "Chavrie" goat cheese with herbs
3 Tbsp sesame seeds

Makes 5 Servings	
Analysis per Serving:	
Carbs	**2.2g**
Calories	76.6
Fat	6.3g
Protein	3.7g

1. Toast sesame seeds by heating them in a dry frying pan on medium/high heat until golden brown. Stir frequently or constantly. Remove from heat and place on a small plate. Let cool completely before continuing.

2. Oil hands with cooking oil to prevent cheese from sticking to hands.

3. Scoop up a small amount of the goat cheese and form into a ball in the palm of your hand. Place on plate with sesame and roll to coat. Repeat. This should make about 10 balls depending on how big you make them.

4. Refrigerate for 30 minute or more. Serve on a platter.

Chile Con Queso

1 cup heavy cream
1/2 cup salsa
1 lb cheddar cheese
1 can green chilies, diced
1/4 tsp garlic salt
1/4 tsp chili powder, optional
1 Tbsp cilantro, finely minced

Makes 16 Servings	
Analysis per Serving:	
Carbs	**1.6g**
Calories	168.9
Fat	15.0g
Protein	7.5g

Use a double boiler. Add all ingredients. Heat while stirring constantly until smooth. Serve warm.

This can be served as a dip with pork rinds or used as a sauce. It's wonderful over scrambled eggs.

Crab Dip

1 cup sour cream
1 Tbsp scallions, chopped
1 can crab meat
1/4 tsp lemon extract
1 dash Worcestershire sauce

Makes 6 Servings	
Analysis per Serving:	
Carbs	**1.7g**
Calories	105.0
Fat	8.3g
Protein	5.9g

Mix all ingredient and serve with pork rinds or stuffed in celery, mushrooms or endive.

Cubed Ham with Horseradish Sauce

1 lb cooked ham
10 small cocktail dill pickles
10 cherry peppers

SAUCE
1/2 cup mayonnaise
2 Tbsp horseradish, to taste
1 tsp Dijon mustard

Makes 10 Servings	
Analysis per Serving:	
Carbs	**2.1g**
Calories	188.8
Fat	14.2g
Protein	8.2g

In selecting your cooked ham, be sure to read the label. Some hams have been cooked with honey or have sugar added. These have 1 to 3g carbs per ounce. Find a cooked ham that has zero carbs. Also read the labels when selecting cocktail dill pickles and the cherry peppers, they vary quite a lot. Select brands that have a serving size of 2 pieces for 1g carbs.

1. Cut ham into about 20 cubes, cutting away rind as you go. Place tooth pick into each cube or simply provide a decorative container of tooth picks.

2. Mix mayonnaise, horseradish and mustard until smooth. Place in a small decorative bowl in center of serving platter.

3. Arrange ham, pickles and cherry peppers on platter. Serve.

One serving is 2 cubes of ham dipped in sauce, 1 pickle and 1 cherry pepper. You can have as much ham as you desire but each cocktail pickle and cherry pepper are about 1/2g carbs each, which can add up fast, so be careful with them.

Feel free to garnish ham or sauce with a sprinkle of paprika and/or chopped parsley for a more decorative look.

Grilled Sausage with Mustard

2 mild Italian sausage, grilled
1/4 cup mustard
10 tooth picks

Makes 10 Servings	
Analysis per Serving:	
Carbs	**0.5g**
Calories	29.0
Fat	2.8g
Protein	1.1g

Grill or broil sausage; cut into 10 pieces and pierce each with tooth picks, accompanied with favorite spicy mustard.

Guacamole

2 avocado, ripe
2 Tbsp salsa
1 Tbsp lemon juice
1/2 tsp garlic salt
1 bunch cilantro, chopped

Makes 8 Servings	
Analysis per Serving:	
Carbs	**7.3g**
Calories	96.5
Fat	7.9g
Protein	1.8g

Scoop out avocado and mashed well. Add all ingredients and mix. Serve with pork rinds or as a side with fajitas.

When storing in the refrigerator, put avocado seed in center and cover with plastic wrap, pushing wrap down onto top surface of guacamole, to eliminate air pockets. This will prevent browning.

Note: Be sure to read the label on the salsa, not all are low in carbs.

Marinated Mushroom & Artichokes

2 lbs mushrooms
2 cans artichoke hearts, drained
3/4 cup water
1/4 cup olive oil
1 clove garlic, chopped
1/4 tsp peppercorns
1/4 tsp ground thyme
1/4 cup cider vinegar
2 Tbsp salt
1/4 tsp dried basil
1 Tbsp bay leaf
1/2 tsp lemon extract

Makes 16 Servings	
Analysis per Serving:	
Carbs	**1.7g**
Calories	37.1
Fat	3.4g
Protein	0.4g

1. Slice mushrooms in half through stems. Quarter artichoke hearts. Combine artichoke hearts and mushrooms.

2. Combine remaining ingredients and heat, but do not boil. Pour over mushrooms and artichoke hearts. Refrigerate overnight.

3. Remove peppercorns and bay leaf before serving.

Portabella Mushrooms with Brie & Pesto

2 portobella mushrooms
1 Tbsp butter
1 Tbsp sherry
1 garlic clove
6 oz brie cheese
2 Tbsp pesto sauce

Makes 2 Servings	
Analysis per Serving:	
Carbs	**4.1g**
Calories	450.0
Fat	36.8g
Protein	22.6g

1. Lightly sauté mushrooms in butter, sherry and garlic on medium heat. Drain on paper towel.

2. Cut up brie into 12 pieces (I like the rind but it can also be removed) and place in mushrooms. Add a ½ tsp of the pesto on top of each.

3. Place under the broiler until cheese melts (usually less than 1 minute). Serve immediately.

Salmon Rolls

1/4 lb lox
4 oz cream cheese
1 Tbsp lemon juice
1 Tbsp capers

Makes 4 Servings	
Analysis per Serving:	
Carbs	**1.1g**
Calories	133.4
Fat	11.1g
Protein	7.3g

1. Let cream cheese come to room temperature or soften in microwave.

2. Combine cream cheese with lemon juice and capers. Spread on salmon slices and roll up firmly.

3. Chill and slice into bite-sized pieces (about 12 - 16).

Salmon Stuffed Mushrooms

10 large mushroom
1 Tbsp butter
1 Tbsp sherry
6 oz salmon, canned
4 oz cream cheese
1 Tbsp dill weed, fresh

Makes 5 Servings	
Analysis per Serving:	
Carbs	**2.5g**
Calories	230.7
Fat	13.9g
Protein	22.8g

1. Lightly sauté mushrooms in butter and sherry on medium heat. Drain and cool on paper towel.

2. Drain can of salmon. Soften cream cheese by leaving it out for one hour or by 20 seconds in the microwave. Mix salmon and cream cheese.

3. Spoon salmon mixture into mushroom and garnish with dill. Refrigerate at least 1 hour then serve.

Salsa & Cream Cheese Dip

8 oz cream cheese
3 Tbsp salsa

Makes 6 Servings	
Analysis per Serving:	
Carbs	**7.4g**
Calories	160.4
Fat	13.5g
Protein	4.3g

Soften cream cheese in microwave. Mix in salsa. Serve with pork rinds or stuffed in celery, mushrooms, or endive.

Note: Be sure to read the label on the salsa, not all are low in carbs.

Sister Cream Cheese

8 oz cream cheese
2 scallions chopped
1 garlic clove, finely chopped
8 green olives w/pimento, chopped
6 walnut halves, chopped
1/4 tsp black pepper, coarsely ground

Makes 8 Servings	
Analysis per Serving:	
Carbs	**2.3g**
Calories	390.9
Fat	37.0g
Protein	13.7g

1. Soften cream cheese (place in microwave).

2. Coarsely chop olives and walnuts. Mix all ingredients together.

Serve on Alpine Bakery flat bread, endive leaf or on squares of cut bell peppers. Stuff in celery, mushrooms or hollowed out cherry tomatoes. It can also be rolled up in roasted red bell peppers (pat dry) secured with a tooth pick. For a light lunch, I like to roll it up in a thin slice of roast beef, ham, turkey or a fresh leaf of lettuce.

Please note that most of these serving methods add carbs, so be careful what you choose and how much you eat.

This is one of my favorite appetizer to bring to a party, it always gets many praises. I often cut up a green or red bell pepper into 8 squares (patted dry) and place a serving of the Sister Cream Cheese on each. This will add about 1g carbs per serving.

Notes:
1. Red onions are also good here, for a stronger taste. Or try a bit of each for a nice medley of colors.
2. Many other nuts can be substituted, such as pine nuts, macadamia nuts, pecans, or even cashews.
3. This recipe comes from a boyfriend I had many, many years ago. He named it, but I have long since forgotten the story behind the name.

Smoked Clam Dip

1 can smoked clams, chopped
1 cup sour cream
2 Tbsp scallions, chopped
1 dash Worcestershire sauce
1/4 tsp paprika

Makes 6 Servings	
Analysis per Serving:	
Carbs	**3.6g**
Calories	124.1
Fat	8.6g
Protein	8.1g

Mix all ingredients and serve with pork rinds or stuffed in celery, mushroom or endive.

Spicy Deviled Eggs

5 eggs
1 Tbsp mayonnaise
1 Tbsp salsa
10 sprigs cilantro

Makes 5 Servings	
Analysis per Serving:	
Carbs	**2.7g**
Calories	105.0
Fat	7.5g
Protein	7.1g

1. Hard boil eggs (bring to a boil and then 8 minutes on medium heat). Let cool.

2. Peel eggs and slice long wise. Gently remove yolks and place in small bowl. Add mayonnaise to yolks and blend well. Add salsa and blend well. Spoon yolk mixture into hollow of eggs whites. Add sprigs of cilantro for a garnish.

Note: Very fresh eggs, when hard boiled, are difficult to peel. Use your oldest eggs first. Usually 1 week or more after purchase is best. Also, if you over-cook the eggs the yolks will turn gray.

Spinach Dip

1 pkg frozen chopped spinach,
   thawed and drained
1 cup sour cream
1 cup mayonnaise
2 Tbsp Parmesan cheese
1/2 pkg Knorr vegetable soup mix
1 Tbsp onion, finely chopped
8 oz waterchestnuts, chopped

Makes 12 Servings	
Analysis per Serving:	
Carbs	**8.2g**
Calories	209.0
Fat	20.0g
Protein	2.7g

Mix all ingredients and refrigerate overnight.

Teriyaki Wings

24 chicken wings
1/2 cup soy sauce
1/2 cup rice vinegar
1/2 cup sesame oil
2 garlic cloves, crushed
1 Tbsp ginger root, grated
1 packet Sweet 'n Low®

Makes 8 Servings	
Analysis per Serving:	
Carbs	**2.8g**
Calories	733.1
Fat	56.8g
Protein	50.5g

1. Mix all ingredients except wings in a large bowl.

2. Rinse and dry wings. Place wings in marinade and refrigerate for at least 1 hour (over night is better).

3. Bake wings at 400°F for 20 minutes. Pour off any liquids. Baste with marinate and broil until brown (5-10 minutes). Turn over, baste and broil again.

Tomato & Mozzarella

8 oz mozzarella cheese
2 tomato, sliced
2 Tbsp pesto sauce
2 basil leaves, sliced

Makes 8 Servings	
Analysis per Serving:	
Carbs	**5.4g**
Calories	443.6
Fat	35.1g
Protein	27.2g

Cut cheese into 8 one oz rounds. Slice tomatoes into 8 thin slices. Stack tomato on cheese. Top with a dab of pesto and garnish with a thin slice of fresh basil. Serve.

Makes a nice side dish too.

Salads

SALADS

Artichoke Salad
Broccoli Sesame Salad
Broccoli Cheddar Salad
Caesar Salad
Chinese Cucumber Salad
Chinese Hot-and-Spicy Asparagus Salad
Cole Slaw
Cottage Cheese & Chile Salad
Crab Salad in Tomato Baskets
Cucumber Lemon Beef Salad
Curried Chicken Salad
Dilled Cucumber Salad
Fiesta Salad
Ham Salad
Marinated Cucumber Salad
Mother & Child Reunion (Chicken & Egg Salad)
Mozzarella Pesto Salad
Oriental Chicken Salad
Radish Salad
Salad with Bacon
Salmon Mousse
Shrimp Louis Salad
Shrimp Salad - Marinated
Spinach & Mushroom Salad
Sweet & Sour Slaw
Syrian Salad
Tofu & Vegetable Salad
Turkey Salad
Turkey Walnut Salad

Artichoke Salad

1 can artichoke hearts, marinated
2 Tbsp red bell pepper, chopped
1/4 cup red onion, sliced
4 oz mushroom caps
4 oz Greek olives, pitted
3 Tbsp pesto sauce
1 Tbsp heavy cream
1 Tbsp red wine vinegar
2 oz feta cheese, crumbled
   salt and pepper, to taste

Makes 6 Servings	
Analysis per Serving:	
Carbs	**4.7g**
Calories	99.0
Fat	7.5g
Protein	3.7g

1. Mix pesto, cream and vinegar until smooth. Cut artichokes into bite sized pieces. Half mushrooms, if desired.

2. Mix all ingredients, except feta cheese, until well coated. Crumble in feta cheese and serve.

Broccoli Sesame Salad

1 head broccoli
2 Tbsp olive oil
1/4 cup rice wine vinegar
1/4 cup soy sauce
2 Tbsp sesame oil
4 Tbsp sesame seeds, toasted

Makes 4 Servings	
Analysis per Serving:	
Carbs	**5.6g**
Calories	189.2
Fat	18.0g
Protein	3.2g

Set oven to 450°F

1. Wash broccoli, discarding leaves and toughest part of stem. Blanch entire head in boiling water for one minute. Rinse under cold water. Break off florets and cut remaining stem (peeled, if desired) into 2" pieces.

2. Pour olive oil onto a baking sheet. Spread broccoli pieces in one layer, turning to coat with olive oil. Roast at 450°F for 5 minutes, turn broccoli pieces over, and continue roasting until broccoli begins to brown, about 5 minute more.

3. Meanwhile, whisk together soy sauce, vinegar, and sesame oil. Stir in 3 Tbsp toasted sesame seeds.

4. When broccoli is done, transfer to a bowl and pour dressing over it, stirring gently to coat. Sprinkle with remaining Tbsp sesame seeds.

You can serve this salad warm or at room temperature. It's OK chilled too.

Broccoli Cheddar Salad

3 cups broccoli, chopped
1/2 cup cheddar cheese, grated
1/2 cup red onion, thinly sliced
3 Tbsp bacon bits

Dressing:
3/4 cup mayonnaise
1 packet Sweet 'n Low®, or less, to taste
1 Tbsp vinegar

Makes 4 Servings	
Analysis per Serving:	
Carbs	**7.1g**
Calories	400.5
Fat	41.1g
Protein	8.0g

1. Lightly steam broccoli for 1 minute. Drain and place in freezer to cool (approx. 1 minute) while preparing the remainder of the salad.

2. Mix mayonnaise, sweetener and vinegar.

3. Combine broccoli, cheese, onions and bacon. Toss. Add the dressing, toss again and serve.

Caesar Salad

1 head romaine lettuce, washed
1 egg
2 tsp anchovy paste
2 garlic cloves, crushed
1/2 tsp Dijon mustard
2/3 cup olive oil
1 Tbsp lemon juice, (~1/2 lemon)
1/4 tsp worcestershire sauce
1/4 tsp fresh ground black pepper
1/3 cup Parmesan cheese, coarsely grated

Makes 4 Servings	
Analysis per Serving:	
Carbs	**4.8g**
Calories	320.5
Fat	31.0g
Protein	7.4g

1. Place egg in boiling water for 1 minute then plunging it into cold water to stop the cooking. Separate the egg, discarding the whites and placing the yolk in a small non-metallic mixing bowl. Beat egg yolk.

2. Add anchovy past, oil, mustard, garlic, lemon juice, worcestershire sauce and pepper. Mix well. Chill dressing for 15 or 20 minutes to allow flavors to meld.

3. Wash and tear lettuce into bite size pieces. Pour dressing over lettuce and toss. Sprinkle with Parmesan cheese and serve immediately.

Notes:
1. Try adding crumbled bacon for no added carbs.
2. Add grilled chicken or salmon fillets to make a full meal - with no added carbs.
3. I think anchovies are disgusting, but the anchovy paste is easy to use and is what really makes this dressing great. You can leave out the anchovy paste if you wish (but then add some salt) but it's not nearly as wonderful.
4. This just might be the best Caesar salad you have ever had!

Chinese Cucumber Salad

3 cucumbers
1 tsp salt
2 Tbsp soy sauce
1/2 cup rice wine vinegar
1 packet Sweet 'n Low®
1 tsp sesame oil
1 Tbsp fresh ginger root, finely chopped

Makes 8 Servings	
Analysis per Serving:	
Carbs	**9.1g**
Calories	75.1
Fat	0.9g
Protein	5.3g

Peel cucumbers. Slice thinly. Mix remaining ingredients and pour over cucumbers. Stir carefully. Chill for 20 minutes and serve.

Chinese Hot & Spicy Asparagus Salad

1 lb asparagus
1 Tbsp minced garlic
1 Tbsp grated ginger root
1/2 tsp salt or herbal salt substitute
1 packet Sweet 'n Low® sweetener
2 Tbsp soy or tamari sauce
1 tsp dark sesame oil
1 Tbsp rice vinegar
1/8 tsp cayenne pepper
1/4 tsp hot-pepper flakes (optional)

Makes 4 Servings	
Analysis per Serving:	
Carbs	**7.3g**
Calories	49.2
Fat	1.3g
Protein	3.4g

1. Bring a large pot of water to a boil over high heat. Trim ends of asparagus and slice each stalk diagonally into 3-inch pieces. Steam until tender (6 to 10 minutes). Drain.

2. In a large bowl combine garlic, ginger root, salt, sweetener, soy sauce, sesame oil, vinegar, cayenne, and hot-pepper flakes. Toss with asparagus. Chill or serve warm.

Cole Slaw

1/2 head cabbage, shredded
1/2 cup mayonnaise
  2 Tbsp heavy cream
  2 Tbsp vinegar
  2 dashes onion salt
  1 packet Sweet 'n Low® sweetener

Makes 3 Servings	
Analysis per Serving:	
Carbs	**4.7g**
Calories	169.6
Fat	17.6g
Protein	1.4g

1. Dressing: Mix all ingredient except cabbage thoroughly.

2. Shred cabbage into thin strips (I like to use a mix of green and red cabbage).

3. Pour dressing over cabbage. Chill for at least 1 hour then serve. Keeps for 2 or 3 days.

Cottage Cheese & Chilies Salad

15 oz cottage cheese
  7 oz green chilies, canned & chopped
1/8 tsp cumin powder
  1 fresh tomato, cut into 8 wedges
  3 Tbsp Italian salad dressing

Makes 4 Servings	
Analysis per Serving:	
Carbs	**9.9g**
Calories	168.1
Fat	7.7g
Protein	15.7g

1. Combine cottage cheese, chilies, cumin and salad dressing. Toss.

2. Place cottage cheese mixture on 4 salad plates. Place two tomato wedges per plate.

3. Chill and serve.

Crab Salad in Tomato Basket

3 cups crab meat
1/2 cup Chinese cabbage, shredded
1 Tbsp grated red onion
2 tsp toasted sesame seed
2 Tbsp fresh cilantro, minced
1/3 cup rice vinegar
1 packet Sweet 'n Low® sweetener
1 Tbsp tamari or soy sauce
2 tsp grated ginger root
1 Tbsp dark sesame oil
1 tsp herbal salt substitute
3 ripe tomatoes

Makes 6 Servings	
Analysis per Serving:	
Carbs	**4.2g**
Calories	109.0
Fat	3.7g
Protein	14.6g

1. In a large bowl combine crab meat, cabbage, onion, sesame seed, and cilantro. Toss well.

2. In another bowl whisk together vinegar, sweetener, tamari, ginger root, oil, and salt substitute. Pour over crab meat mixture and toss well.

3. Cut each tomato in half width-wise. With a sharp knife, score interior and scoop out pulp to form a shell. Fill each with a generous portion of crab salad and place on lettuce-lined platter.

Cucumber Lemon Beef Salad

1 lb lean rare roast beef, thinly sliced
1 cup English cucumber, thinly sliced
1/2 small red onion, thinly sliced
2 Tbsp capers, drained
1/4 cup parsley, chopped

Lemon Dressing:
1/4 tsp lemon extract
 1 clove garlic, minced
1/2 tsp salt
1/2 packet Sweet 'n Low®
1/2 tsp fresh ginger root, grated
 1 tsp Dijon mustard
1/4 cup salad oil

Makes 4 Servings	
Analysis per Serving:	
Carbs	**3.5g**
Calories	381.3
Fat	30.0g
Protein	23.2g

1. Lemon Dressing: In a small bowl combine lemon juice, garlic, salt, sweetener, lemon extract, ginger, and mustard. Using a whisk or fork, gradually beat in oil. Makes about 1/3 cup.

2. Combine beef, cucumber, and onion. Mix lightly with Lemon Dressing and capers; cover and refrigerate for 1 to 3 hours to blend flavors.

3. To serve, mix in parsley. Heap salad in a shallow bowl or on a platter lined with lettuce.

Curried Chicken Salad

1/2 cup mayonnaise
  1 Tbsp lemon juice
  2 Tbsp curry powder
  1 cooked chicken
1/4 cup diced celery
1/4 cup almond slivers

Makes 4 Servings	
Analysis per Serving:	
Carbs	**3.8g**
Calories	312.2
Fat	29.2g
Protein	13.1g

1. Remove meat from chicken and cut into bite sized pieces.

2. Blend mayonnaise, lemon juice, and curry powder.

3. Mix all ingredients. Chill at least one hour before serving.

Dilled Cucumber Salad

  1 cup cucumber, peeled & diced
  1 pint sour cream
  1 Tbsp white wine vinegar
1/2 tsp salt
1/8 tsp cayenne
  1 Tbsp onion, grated
  3 Tbsp fresh dill, chopped

Makes 4 Servings	
Analysis per Serving:	
Carbs	**6.1g**
Calories	251.6
Fat	24.1g
Protein	3.9g

Mix sour cream, vinegar, salt, cayenne, and grated onion. Stir in chopped dill and diced cucumber. Refrigerate two hours before serving.

Fiesta Salad

1 head romaine lettuce
3 oz cheddar cheese, shredded
3 oz Monterey jack cheese, shredded
4 chicken breasts, grilled
4 tbsp guacamole
1 tomato, chopped
1/4 red onion, chopped
2 oz black olives, chopped or sliced
1/4 cup ranch salad dressing
1/4 cup salsa

Makes 4 Servings	
Analysis per Serving:	
Carbs	**9.8g**
Calories	938.9
Fat	59.0g
Protein	89.0g

1. Wash and tear lettuce. Arrange on 4 plates.

2. On 1 side of plate, make a line of cheddar cheese and use Monterey Jack on the other side.

3. Cut grilled chicken breasts into bite sized pieces and place between the two cheeses.

4. Place 1 tablespoon of guacamole in center of each plate. Sprinkle tomato, red onions and black olives over each salad.

5. Mix ranch dressing and salsa together. Serve on the side or drizzle over each salad.

Ham Salad

1 cup cooked ham, chopped
1 Tbsp pickle relish
1 Tbsp Dijon mustard
3 Tbsp mayonnaise

Makes 4 Servings	
Analysis per Serving:	
Carbs	**1.6g**
Calories	145.4
Fat	12.6g
Protein	6.5g

Combine all ingredients and stir well. Serve.

Marinated Cucumber Salad

1 large cucumber, peeled and sliced
1 Tbsp wine vinegar
1 Tbsp balsamic vinegar
1 Tbsp olive oil
1 Tbsp red onion, thinly sliced
1 dash garlic salt
1 Tbsp cilantro, chopped

Makes 3 Servings	
Analysis per Serving:	
Carbs	**6.8g**
Calories	70.4
Fat	4.8g
Protein	1.6g

Mix all ingredients. Refrigerate 1 hour. Serve.

Mother & Child Reunion (Chicken & Egg Salad)

1 chicken, cooked
4 eggs, hard boiled
1/2 cup Ranch salad dressing
2 scallions, chopped
    salt & pepper, to taste

Makes 4 Servings	
Analysis per Serving:	
Carbs	**3.6g**
Calories	292.6
Fat	22.6g
Protein	18.7g

1. Take meat off the bone and cut into bite size pieces.

2. Mix thoroughly, all ingredients except for the eggs.

3. Chop the eggs and gently mix with chicken. Serve on a bed of lettuce.

Note: Most people love this salad, although some are appalled by the name I have given it. I think it's quite funny!

Mozzarella Pesto Salad

4 oz mozzarella cheese, fresh
2 Tbsp red bell pepper, minced
1 Tbsp pesto sauce
1 Tbsp heavy cream
    salt and pepper, to taste

Makes 2 Servings	
Analysis per Serving:	
Carbs	**6.8g**
Calories	805.7
Fat	62.3g
Protein	51.0g

1. Mix pesto with cream until smooth.

2. Cube fresh mozzarella cheese, add bell pepper. Mix well with pesto. Serve.

Oriental Chicken Salad

1 chicken, cooked
3 scallions, minced
4 ribs of bok choy, chopped
2 tsp hot pepper flakes
1/4 cup peanuts, roasted
1/4 cup cilantro, chopped
2/3 cup Lauri's oriental dressing

Makes 4 Servings	
Analysis per Serving:	
Carbs	**6.3g**
Calories	296.5
Fat	24.5g
Protein	15.1g

Remove chicken meat from bones and cut into bite sized pieces. Mix together all ingredients and serve. Keeps for 2 or 3 days.

Notes:
1. Use left-over chicken or whole roasted chicken.
2. If you do not like spicy food then omit pepper flacks and substitute minced red bell pepper.

Radish Salad

1 cup radishes, sliced
1/2 cup mung bean sprouts, fresh
1 Tbsp green bell pepper, minced
1 Tbsp cilantro or parsley, minced
1 tsp chives, fresh & chopped
1/4 cup salad oil
1 Tbsp lemon juice
1 tsp soy sauce

Makes 2 Servings	
Analysis per Serving:	
Carbs	**5.2g**
Calories	265.6
Fat	27.6g
Protein	1.6g

Whisk together oil, lemon juice and soy sauce. Add all other ingredients. Toss and serve.

Salad with Bacon

1 head romaine lettuce
1 lb bacon, cooked
1 cup mayonnaise
1 Tbsp wine vinegar
1/4 cup Parmesan cheese
1/4 cup scallion, chopped

Makes 4 Servings	
Analysis per Serving:	
Carbs	**4.7g**
Calories	1094.9
Fat	104.4g
Protein	39.6g

1. Mix mayonnaise and vinegar.

2. Tear lettuce leaves. Toss together lettuce, bacon and mayonnaise.

3. Sprinkle on the Parmesan cheese and scallions. Toss just before serving.

Salmon Mousse

2 envelopes unflavored gelatin
1/2 cup cold water
3 Tbsp lemon juice
2 cups salmon, cooked, flaked
1 tsp minced onion
1 cup mayonnaise
    dash Tabasco sauce

Makes 6 Servings	
Analysis per Serving:	
Carbs	**3.6g**
Calories	417.0
Fat	33.9g
Protein	29.8g

1. Empty envelopes of gelatin in cold water, soak for 5 minutes. Heat water until gelatin is completely dissolved. Add lemon juice. Cool.

2. Mix together flaked salmon, onion, mayonnaise, and Tabasco. Fold into gelatin mixture. Pour into fish mold. Chill until set; unmold. Slice and serve on lettuce.

Shrimp Louis Salad

2 cups small shrimp, cooked & shelled
1 scallion, chopped
Dressing:
1/2 cup mayonnaise
1 Tbsp ketchup
1 Tbsp dill pickle relish

Makes 2 Servings	
Analysis per Serving:	
Carbs	**3.7g**
Calories	511.2
Fat	48.6g
Protein	21.2g

1. Make dressing by mixing well the mayonnaise, ketchup and relish.

2. Toss shrimp, scallions and dressing. Chill and serve.

Note: Check your labels when choosing your relish. Avoid sweet pickle relishes which are high in carbs. Your dill pickle relish should be 1g carb per tablespoon or less.

Shrimp Salad - Marinated

1 lb fresh shrimp, cooked & peeled
2 Tbsp green bell pepper, minced
1 Tbsp scallions, minced
1 clove garlic, minced
1 1/2 Tbsp fresh parsley, minced
1/4 tsp lemon extract
1 cup Lauri's oriental dressing
1/4 tsp salt
1 dash black pepper

Makes 4 Servings	
Analysis per Serving:	
Carbs	**6.8g**
Calories	385.9
Fat	29.4g
Protein	24.2g

Place shrimp, scallions and peppers in a deep ceramic or glass bowl. Mix remaining ingredients thoroughly and pour over shrimp mixture. Cover and marinate in refrigerator for 24 hours before serving, stirring occasionally.

Spinach & Mushroom Salad

10 oz fresh spinach, washed & chopped
10 whole fresh mushrooms, sliced
 4 hard-boiled eggs, chopped
 6 slices bacon, cooked & crumbled
Dressing:
 1 cup olive oil
1/4 cup sour cream
1/4 cup red wine vinegar
1/2 tsp dry mustard
 1 packet Sweet 'n Low®
 1 tsp salt
1/4 tsp black pepper

Makes 8 Servings	
Analysis per Serving:	
Carbs	**7.6g**
Calories	480.1
Fat	48.1g
Protein	7.5g

Toss spinach, mushrooms, chopped egg, and crumbled bacon. Whisk remaining ingredients together. Toss with vegetables to coat spinach.

Sweet & Sour Slaw

1/2 head cabbage
1/4 cup sesame oil
  1 Tbsp vinegar
  2 tsp ginger root, fresh grated
1/4 onion, sliced thin
  1 garlic clove, crushed
  1 packet Sweet 'n Low®

Makes 6 Servings	
Analysis per Serving:	
Carbs	**9.9g**
Calories	126.2
Fat	9.5g
Protein	1.8g

1. Shred cabbage into thin strips (I like to use a mix of green cabbage, bok choy and Chinese cabbage). Set aside.

2. Lightly sauté onions, garlic & ginger in 1 Tbsp oil for 1 minute. Add remaining oil, vinegar, soy sauce and heat for 1 minute.

3. Remove from heat, add Sweet'n Low, and stir.

4. Pour dressing, while still hot, over cabbage and mix thoroughly. Let cool for 1 minute. Drain off excess liquid. Chill for at least 1 hour then serve.

Keeps for 2 or 3 days.

Syrian Salad

1 head romaine lettuce
1 cucumber, thinly sliced
6 radishes, thinly sliced
1/2 red bell pepper, thinly sliced
1/2 green bell pepper, thinly sliced
1/4 cup red onion, thinly sliced
2 scallion, chopped
4 oz feta cheese, crumbled
2 oz black olives, sliced
2 Tbsp capers
1/2 cup parsley, chopped

DRESSING
1/3 cup olive oil
1 Tbsp lemon juice
1 garlic clove
1/4 tsp dried mint flakes
    salt and pepper to taste

1. Wash and tear lettuce into bite size pieces and place in large salad bowl (or 8 individual salad plates).

2. Arrange vegetables on top in an attractive manner. Top with feta, black olives and capers.

3. Combine olive oil, lemon juice, garlic, mint and salt & pepper. Let dressing sit for 15 minutes, then drizzle over salad. Serve.

Tofu & Vegetable Salad

16 oz tofu
1 fennel bulb
1 green bell pepper
1 red bell pepper
4 celery stalk
1/2 red onion

Marinade:
1 cup salad oil
1/3 cup red wine vinegar
1/3 cup water
2 Tbsp soy sauce
1 tsp lime juice
1/2 tsp garlic salt
1/2 tsp ginger, ground
1 tsp fennel seed

Makes 8 Servings	
Analysis per Serving:	
Carbs	**7.3g**
Calories	310.5
Fat	30.2g
Protein	5.7g

1. Cut fennel bulb, peppers, celery and onion into match-stick sized pieces.

2. Cut tofu into bite size cubes. Place tofu and vegetables in a glass bowl.

3. Whisk together all the marinate ingredients. Pour over vegetables & tofu, toss. Marinate in refrigerator for 24 hours or at least over night. Serve.

Turkey Salad

1 lb smoked turkey, cut into thin strips
1/4 lb jack cheese, cut into thin strips
1/3 cup red bell pepper, diced
2 Tbsp green onions, chopped
1/3 cup mayonnaise
1/3 cup sour cream
1 Tbsp prepared horseradish
   freshly ground pepper, to taste

Makes 4 Servings	
Analysis per Serving:	
Carbs	**2.8g**
Calories	430.7
Fat	32.5g
Protein	33.0g

1. In a large bowl toss together turkey, cheese, bell pepper, and green onions.

2. In a separate bowl blend mayonnaise, sour cream, and horseradish.

3. Add dressing to turkey mixture; gently toss to coat. Season liberally with pepper.

Turkey Walnut Salad

2 cups cooked turkey
1/2 cup walnuts, chopped
2 celery ribs
1/2 cup mayonnaise
   salt & pepper, to taste

Makes 2 Servings	
Analysis per Serving:	
Carbs	**5.2g**
Calories	828.3
Fat	71.4g
Protein	49.6g

1. Cube turkey and dice celery.

2. Mix turkey, celery, walnuts and mayonnaise. Serve.

Notes:
1. This salad is great for left-over turkey from Thanksgiving.
2. You can substitute pecan, almond, cashews or most any other nut for about that same carbs.

Vegetables

VEGETABLES

Asparagus with Hollandaise Sauce
Broccoli Sesame
Broccoli with Lemon Ginger Sauce
Cabbage with Bacon
Cauliflower with Cheese Sauce
Cauliflower with Spicy Peanut Sauce
Creamed Spinach
Green Beans Almondine
Grilled Asparagus with Bacon
Mixed Vegetables with Pesto Sauce
Mock Mashed Potatoes
Roasted Peppers
Sautéed Mushrooms
Spaghetti Squash
Spicy Green Beans
Summer Squash - Microwave
Vegetables Alfredo
Zucchini Parmesan

Asparagus with Hollandaise Sauce

24 asparagus spears
1/2 red bell pepper, sliced thin

Sauce:
   3 egg yolks, beaten
   3 Tbsp boiling water
   2 tsp lemon juice
   1 tsp sherry
   1 tsp tarragon vinegar
1/2 cup butter
1/4 tsp salt
   dash cayenne pepper

Makes 3 Servings	
Analysis per Serving:	
Carbs	**6.9g**
Calories	360.4
Fat	35.7g
Protein	5.9g

1. Steam asparagus and red bell pepper. Prepare sauce while veggies are steaming.

2. Slowing heat and keep warm butter, lemon juice, sherry, vinegar, salt and cayenne.

3. Over a double boiler, warm egg yolks, while stirring constantly with a wire whisk. When yolks start to thicken, add 1 tablespoon at a time of boiling water, stirring constantly with wire whisk. When thicken remove from heat and whisk into the butter mixture. Serve immediately.

Notes:
1. Makes about 1 cup.
2. You can use the "Quick & Easy" Hollandaise sauce instead (see Sauces & Salad Dressings).

Broccoli Sesame

1 head broccoli
1 Tbsp sesame oil
1 Tbsp sesame seeds, toasted
1 Tbsp water
1 Tbsp rice vinegar
1 tsp lemon juice
1 tsp soy sauce
1/2 tsp ground ginger

Makes 3 Servings	
Analysis per Serving:	
Carbs	**3.1g**
Calories	68.7
Fat	6.1g
Protein	1.5g

1. Wash and cut broccoli. Let drip dry.

2. Heat oil in large skillet on medium/high heat. Add broccoli and stir to coat broccoli with oil. Cover and cook for 2 or 3 minutes, stirring frequently.

3. Mix water, vinegar, lemon juice, soy sauce and ginger. Pour over broccoli. Stir, cover, reduce heat to medium and cook 3 more minutes or until desired tenderness.

4. Place on serving dish. Sprinkle with toasted sesame seeds, toss. Serve immediately.

Broccoli with Lemon Ginger Sauce

1 head broccoli

1/2 cup mayonnaise
2 Tbsp heavy cream
2 Tbsp lemon juice
1/4 tsp ground ginger
    salt and white pepper, to taste

Makes 2 Servings	
Analysis per Serving:	
Carbs	**4.2g**
Calories	462.4
Fat	52.4g
Protein	2.3g

1. Wash and cut broccoli into spears. Steam to desired tenderness. Prepare sauce while steaming.

2. Mix mayonnaise, cream, lemon juice, ginger, salt and pepper. Heat slowing and stirring constantly, in a double broiler or over very low heat.

3. Pour sauce over broccoli and serve immediately.

Note: You can use fresh grated ginger (about 1/2 tsp) for a stronger ginger taste but the sauce will not be as smooth.

Cabbage with Bacon

1/2 head cabbage
  6 slices bacon
1/2 cup water
  1 Tbsp red wine vinegar
     salt and pepper, to taste

Makes 3 Servings	
Analysis per Serving:	
Carbs	**8.6g**
Calories	113.1
Fat	6.7g
Protein	6.0g

1. Cut through bacon slices 6 to 8 times. Fry bacon bits on high heat in a skillet until half cooked. Pour off most of the grease.

2. Cut cabbage into bite size pieces. Add to bacon, reduce heat to medium and cook for 2 minutes stirring occasionally. Add water and cover for 5 minutes, stir occasionally. Add more water if it becomes too dry.

3. Toss in vinegar, season to taste & serve.

Cauliflower with Cheese Sauce

1 head cauliflower
1/2 cup heavy cream
1/4 cup water
1/2 lb cheddar cheese, grated
1 tsp Dijon mustard
2 drops worcestershire sauce
dash paprika

Makes 3 Servings	
Analysis per Serving:	
Carbs	**3.9g**
Calories	451.0
Fat	39.9g
Protein	20.4g

1. Wash, cut and steam cauliflower.

2. Meanwhile prepare cheese sauce. In a double boiler (or over very low heat) mix and heat remaining ingredients. Stir frequently until smooth.

3. Pour sauce over cauliflower in serving dish. Serve immediately.

Note: Also try the "Cheese Sauce Mexicana" for a nice variation.

Cauliflower with Spicy Peanut Sauce

1 head cauliflower
1 Tbsp peanut oil, or sesame oil
2 scallion, chopped
2 garlic clove, minced
1 tsp chili powder
3 Tbsp peanut butter, chunky
3 Tbsp water
1 Tbsp soy sauce
1 tsp lime juice
1 packet Sweet 'n Low® sweetener
1/4 tsp pepper
   salt to taste

Makes 4 Servings	
Analysis per Serving:	
Carbs	**6.2g**
Calories	118.7
Fat	9.6g
Protein	4.1g

1. Wash, cut and steam cauliflower. Meanwhile make sauce.

2. In a heavy skillet, heat oil and sauté green onions, garlic and chili power for 1 minute. Add remaining ingredients and mix well as it heats. Add more water if it gets too thick.

3. Pour sauce over cauliflower and serve immediately.

Creamed Spinach

1 packet frozen chopped spinach
1/3 cup heavy cream
   dash garlic salt
   dash nutmeg

Makes 3 Servings	
Analysis per Serving:	
Carbs	**6.9g**
Calories	127.8
Fat	10.3g
Protein	5.0g

1. Defrost spinach in microwave. Drain.

2. Mix all ingredient and return to the microwave for 2 or 3 minutes until heated through.

Note: For a variation, after mixing all ingredients, place in a casserole dish, sprinkle with 1/3 cup of grated Romano cheese and bake for 10 minutes at 350°F. This will add 0.3g carbs per serving.

Green Beans Almondine

1 lb green beans
1/4 cup slivered almonds
 2 Tbsp butter
 1 tsp lemon juice
1/4 tsp salt

Makes 4 Servings	
Analysis per Serving:	
Carbs	**9.5g**
Calories	127.8
Fat	9.6g
Protein	3.6g

1. Steam green beans.

2. Stirring occasionally, cook almonds in butter over low heat just until golden brown (do not burn). Remove almonds from heat and add lemon juice and salt. Stir.

3. Pour almond mixture over green beans and serve.

Grilled Asparagus With Bacon

10 asparagus spears
4 slices bacon
2 Tbsp sour cream

Makes 2 Servings	
Analysis per Serving:	
Carbs	**4.0g**
Calories	120.4
Fat	9.4g
Protein	6.0g

1. Blanch (or par boil) asparagus in boiling water for 1 or 2 minutes depending on how young and fresh the asparagus is.

2. Fry bacon 1/2 or 3/4 towards the way you like it. Drain.

3. Wrap two slices of bacon around 5 spears. Secure with tooth pick if needed. Repeat.

4. Grill asparagus bunches for 1 or 2 minutes per side.

5. Garnish with sour cream and serve.

Alternate garnishes: Hollandaise Sauce, Bearnaise Sauce, Newburg Sauce or Lemon Mayonnaise Sauce.

Mixed Vegetables with Pesto Sauce

1 cup zucchini
1 cup eggplant
1 cup mushroom caps
1 can artichoke bottoms
3 Tbsp butter
3 garlic cloves, minced
1/4 cup heavy cream
3 Tbsp pesto sauce
1/4 cup Parmesan cheese

Makes 4 Servings	
Analysis per Serving:	
Carbs	**6.7g**
Calories	232.7
Fat	21.0g
Protein	5.9g

1. Wash and chop vegetables into bite sized pieces.

2. Heat butter in large skillet. Add garlic and vegetables (but not the artichokes), sauté for 3 minutes or until desired tenderness.

3. Add artichokes, cream and pesto sauce. Stir. Heat for 1 minute.

4. Place vegetables in serving dish. Sprinkle with Parmesan cheese. Serve.

Mock Mashed Potatoes

2 cups cauliflower florets, chopped
1 Tbsp sour cream, more to taste
1 Tbsp butter
  salt and pepper, to taste

Makes 2 Servings	
Analysis per Serving:	
Carbs	**4.8g**
Calories	106.0
Fat	8.9g
Protein	2.5g

1. Steam or microwave cauliflower until <u>very</u> soft.

2. Put cauliflower in blender or food processor with butter and sour cream, blend.

3. Add salt & pepper to taste. Serve hot.

Notes:
1. Frozen cauliflower works very well.
2. Grated cheese, minced chives and/or parsley are nice variations to add. Hand mix these in after blending the cauliflower.

Roasted Red Peppers

4 red bell peppers
1/3 cup olive oil
2 Tbsp balsamic vinegar
3 Tbsp fresh parsley & basil, chopped
1 clove garlic, minced

Makes 8 Servings	
Analysis per Serving:	
Carbs	**9.5g**
Calories	120.9
Fat	9.4g
Protein	2.1g

1. Roast peppers over an open flame or in broiler, turning frequently, until skins are charred and blistered. Place in a plastic bag; close top and let sit 5 to 10 minutes. Remove skins under running water.

2. Cut peppers in half, lengthwise, holding them over a bowl to catch juice. Remove seeds and stem. Tear or cut lengthwise into strips 1/2 to 1 inch wide. Put in a serving bowl or dish.

3. In a small bowl whisk together pepper juice, olive oil, vinegar, herbs, and garlic. Pour over peppers.

4. Serve immediately or marinate at room temperature for several hours.

Time-saver Tip: Recipe can be made a day ahead. Store in the refrigerator, covered. Serve at room temperature.

Sautéed Mushrooms

2 cups mushroom caps, sliced or chopped
1/4 cup parsley, minced
2 garlic cloves, minced
3 Tbsp butter
1 Tbsp dry white wine
  salt and pepper to taste

Makes 2 Servings	
Analysis per Serving:	
Carbs	**5.7g**
Calories	184.7
Fat	17.5g
Protein	2.4g

Heat butter in skillet on medium heat. Add garlic and mushrooms, stir frequently for 2 minutes. Add parsley, stir. Add white wine and stir. Salt & pepper, to taste. Serve.

Note: This can be served as a side vegetable for 2 or great on steaks or pork chops for 4.

Spaghetti Squash

1 spaghetti squash
2 garlic cloves, crushed
2 Tbsp butter
1/2 cup Parmesan cheese

Makes 4 Servings	
Analysis per Serving:	
Carbs	**2.6g**
Calories	106.3
Fat	8.8g
Protein	4.5g

Preheat oven to 375°F

1. Slice the squash in half length wise and scoop out the seeds. Place face down on a buttered tray and bake for 30 minutes at 375°. Cool for 10 or 15 minutes. Remove the insides carefully to maintain long strands.

2. Sauté the garlic in butter for 2 minutes.

3. Lightly toss butter mixture into spaghetti squash. Sprinkle with Parmesan cheese and serve immediately.

Spicy Green Beans

4 cups green beans
1 garlic clove, studded with 3 whole cloves
1/4 yellow onion, chopped
1 bay leaf
2 tsp cider vinegar
1/2 tsp salt
1/4 tsp cinnamon
1/4 tsp cumin

Makes 4 Servings	
Analysis per Serving:	
Carbs	**9.1g**
Calories	39.1
Fat	0.2g
Protein	2.1g

1. Bring 1/2 cup water to a boil. Add garlic, onion, bay leaf and green beans. Reduce heat and simmer for 15 minutes or until beans are tender.

2. Remove garlic clove and bay leaf.

3. Add vinegar, salt, cinnamon and cumin. Cook 1 or 2 more minutes. Serve.

Summer Squash - Microwave

1 crookneck yellow squash, sliced
1 zucchini, sliced
1 tsp Mrs. Dash, Garlic Blend
1 Tbsp butter

Makes 2 Servings	
Analysis per Serving:	
Carbs	**4.5g**
Calories	71.6
Fat	5.9g
Protein	1.4g

1. Arrange sliced squash in a shallow microwavable bowl. Sprinkle with seasoning. Cut pat of butter into 4 pieces and place on top of squash.

2. Cover bowl with wax paper. Cook in microwave for 4 minutes or more. Serve immediately.

Vegetables Alfredo

1 cup broccoli, chopped
1 cup cauliflower, canned
1 cup mushroom caps, chopped
2 Tbsp olive oil
2 garlic cloves, minced
1/2 cup Alfredo sauce
1/2 cup Parmesan cheese, grated

Makes 3 Servings	
Analysis per Serving:	
Carbs	**6.9g**
Calories	225.7
Fat	18.0g
Protein	9.7g

1. Chop vegetables into bite size pieces. Place broccoli into steamer for 3 to 5 minutes or until desired tenderness.

2. Sauté garlic and mushrooms in olive oil for 2 minutes. Drain.

3. Add sauce and steamed vegetables to mushrooms. Stir. Sprinkle on top the Parmesan cheese and serve.

Notes:
1. You can substitute zucchini, yellow squash or asparagus to make nice variations.
2. You can add 1/4 cup chopped fresh basil leaves in the last 30 seconds of sautéed mushrooms, stirring constantly. This adds 0.5g carbs.
3. Sometimes I use grated mozzarella cheese instead of the Parmesan. It's more difficult to eat, due to the stringiness of the cheese - but that can be fun in a casual setting.

Zucchini Parmesan

4 zucchini
2 Tbsp butter
3 garlic clove, minced
1/2 cup Parmesan cheese

Makes 4 Servings	
Analysis per Serving:	
Carbs	**4.9g**
Calories	117.3
Fat	8.9g
Protein	5.9g

1. Wash and cube zucchini. Steam for 3 minutes.

2. Meanwhile, melt butter in sauce pan on medium heat, add garlic and sauté for 1or two minutes (but don't let it burn).

3. Toss garlic butter and Parmesan cheese with steamed zucchini. Serve hot.

Substitute yellow squash, if desired, for same carb count.

Carbohydrates of Vegetables
Grams
1 cup, fresh (unless stated otherwise)

Alfalfa sprouts	1.3	Jicama	15.9
Artichoke hearts	8.8	Lettuce	1.9 - 2.6
Arugala	0.7	Mushrooms	3.3
Asparagus	6.1	Mustard greens	2.7
Avocado, 1 whole	14.9	Okra	7.6
Bean sprouts, mung	4.2	Olives, black, 4 ave.	1.1
Beets	13.0	Olives, green, 4 ave.	0.2
Belgian endive	1.7	Onions, see page 8	
Bell pepper, 1 med.	5.8	Parsnips	23.9
Bell peppers, diced	12.5	Peas	21.0
Bok choy	1.5	Potatoes	43.2
Broccoli	4.6	Pumpkin, canned	19.8
Brussels sprouts	7.9	Radicchio	1.8
Cabbage, green	3.3	Radishes, 4 ave.	0.6
Cabbage, red	3.8	Rhubarb	5.6
Cabbage, Chinese	4.1	Rutabaga	11.4
Carrots	10.2	Snow pea pods	7.4
Cauliflower, cooked	5.2	Soybeans	33.0
Cauliflower, raw	3.9	Spaghetti squash	7.0
Celery	4.4	Spinach	2.0
Chard (leaves only)	8.9	Summer squashes	~5.0
Corn	29.3	Sweet potato	32.3
Cowpeas (black-eye)	100.3	Tomato, med.	5.7
Cucumber, 1 med.	9.6	Turnip	8.0
Eggplant	5.0	Winter squashes	12 - 22.5
Fennel bulb, 1 ave.	17.1	Yellow squash	5.3
Green beans	7.9	Zucchini	3.8

Vegetarian Main Dishes

VEGETARIAN MAIN DISHES

Asparagus & Cheese Soufflé
Cauliflower Cashew Loaf
Green Chili Frittata
Ratatouille
Spaghetti al Pesto
Spaghetti Alfredo
Spaghetti Squash Casserole
Spaghetti with Red Sauce
Spinach Frittata
Spinach Lasagna
Stir Fry Vegetables & Tofu
Teriyaki Tofu
Tofu Italiano
Tofu Stuffed Peppers
Zucchini Boats

Asparagus & Cheese Soufflé

2 cups water
1 cup chopped fresh asparagus
1 cup heavy cream
4 egg yolks, lightly beaten
4 egg whites
2 oz shredded sharp cheddar cheese (1/4 cup)
1/4 tsp salt
1/4 tsp dried dill weed
1/8 tsp coarsely ground pepper

Makes 6 Servings	
Analysis per Serving:	
Carbs	**2.4g**
Calories	199.6
Fat	18.5g
Protein	g6.5

Set oven to 400°F

1. Bring water to a boil in a small saucepan; add asparagus. Cook 3 minutes; drain and set aside.

2. Combine cream and egg yolks in a saucepan, and stir well. Cook 1 minute until thickened, stirring constantly. Add cheese, salt, dill weed and pepper. Stirring until cheese melts.

3. Pour mixture into a bowl; stir in asparagus.

4. Beat egg whites (at room temperature) at high speed of a mixer until stiff peaks form. Stir 1/4 of egg whites into asparagus mixture; fold remaining egg whites into asparagus mixture.

5. Spoon mixture into a 2-quart soufflé dish coated with butter. Place on middle rack of a 400°F oven; immediately reduce temperature to 375°F and bake 40 minutes.

Makes a good side dish too.

Cauliflower Cashew Loaf

1/2 head cauliflower, chopped
3 oz cashews, chopped
3 eggs
2 Tbsp heavy cream
4 oz cheddar cheese, grated
2 scallions, chopped
1/2 tsp garlic salt
1/4 tsp salt and pepper, each
1 tsp cumin
1/2 tsp paprika

Makes 6 Servings	
Analysis per Serving:	
Carbs	**4.5g**
Calories	163.9
Fat	13.2g
Protein	7.8g

Set oven to 350°F

1. Beat eggs with cream and seasonings.

2. Add chopped cauliflower, cashews, green onions, and cheese; mix well.

3. Press cauliflower mixture into greased non-metal bread pan. The more densely pressed the better the loaf will hold together. Bake at 350°F for 45 minutes. Let cool 5 to 10 minutes before cutting and serving.

Makes a great side dish too.

Green Chili Frittata

8 eggs
1/4 cup heavy cream
4 oz green chili peppers, canned, diced
2 Tbsp salsa
1/4 tsp salt
1/4 cup bell pepper, diced
1 Tbsp yellow onion, diced fine
1/2 cup Monterey jack cheese, shredded
1/2 cup cheddar cheese, shredded

Makes 6 Servings	
Analysis per Serving:	
Carbs	**3.5g**
Calories	241.5
Fat	16.7g
Protein	14.9g

Set oven to 350°F

1. Beat the eggs and cream. Add all ingredient except ½ the cheese and blend well.

2. Pour mixture into deep non-metallic pie dish. Sprinkle extra cheese on top. Bake for 40 minutes. Let cool for 5 to 10 minutes. Cut into 6 pieces. Serve at once. Refrigerate left overs.

Ratatouille

1 Tbsp butter
1 Tbsp olive oil
1/2 yellow onion, chopped
4 garlic cloves, crushed
1 eggplant, peeled and cubed
1 zucchini, cubed
1 yellow squash, cubed
1 green bell pepper, sliced
2 Tbsp dry red wine
1 cup Classico Tomato Alfredo Sauce
1 bay leaf
1/2 cup water, if needed

Makes 8 Servings	
Analysis per Serving:	
Carbs	**9.5g**
Calories	88.3
Fat	5.1g
Protein	2.3g

1. Cube vegetables into bite sized pieces.

2. In a large deep skillet, sauté onions in butter on medium/high heat until tender (about 2 minutes). Add olive oil and garlic and sauté 1 minute longer.

3. Add cubed vegetables and sauté for about 5 minutes, stirring frequently.

4. Add wine, pasta sauce and bay leaf. Stir. Reduce heat to medium low and cook for 15 minutes or until eggplant is cooked through well. Stir occasionally, adding water, if needed.

5. Remove bay leaf. Serve immediately.

Spaghetti al Pesto

1 spaghetti squash
1/4 cup pine nuts
2 garlic cloves, crushed
1 Tbsp butter
2 Tbsp pesto sauce
2 Tbsp heavy cream
1/2 cup Parmesan cheese

Makes 2 Servings	
Analysis per Serving:	
Carbs	**9.6g**
Calories	392.7
Fat	34.7g
Protein	16.5g

Preheat oven to 375°F

1. Slice the squash in half length wise and scoop out the seeds. Place face down on a buttered tray and bake for 30 minutes at 375°F. Cool for 10 or 15 minutes. Remove the insides carefully with a fork to maintain long strands.

2. While the squash is baking, toast pine nuts until slightly brown.

3. Sauté the garlic in butter for 2 minutes. Turn off heat. Add cream and pesto sauce and stir.

4. Lightly toss pesto mixture into spaghetti squash. Sprinkle with pine nuts and Parmesan cheese. Serve immediately

Spaghetti Alfredo

1 spaghetti squash
1/2 cup Alfredo sauce
1/4 cup Parmesan cheese

Makes 2 Servings	
Analysis per Serving:	
Carbs	**5.9g**
Calories	152.2
Fat	10.3g
Protein	7.5g

Preheat oven to 375°F

1. Slice the squash in half length wise and scoop out the seeds. Place face down on a buttered tray and bake for 30 minutes at 375°F. Cool for 5 minutes. Remove the insides carefully with a fork to maintain long strands.

2. Heat up Alfredo sauce. Pour over spaghetti squash, sprinkle parmesan cheese on top and serve.

Spaghetti Squash Casserole

1 spaghetti squash
2 scallions, chopped
2 garlic cloves, crushed
1/3 lb mushrooms, fresh & sliced
    salt & pepper, to taste
1 cup ricotta cheese
1 cup mozzarella cheese, grated
1 Tbsp butter
1/2 tsp oregano
2 Tbsp parsley
2 Tbsp basil, fresh & chopped
1 dash thyme
1/2 cup Parmesan cheese

Makes 4 Servings	
Analysis per Serving:	
Carbs	**9.4g**
Calories	298.7
Fat	21.3g
Protein	18.9g

Preheat oven to 375°F

1. Slice the squash in half length wise and scoop out the seeds. Place face down on a buttered tray and bake for 30 minutes at 375°F. Cool for 10 or 15 minutes. Remove the insides carefully with a fork to maintain long strands.

2. While the squash is baking, sauté in butter for 5 minutes the green onions, garlic, mushrooms, salt, pepper and herbs.

3. Combine all ingredients, except parmesan cheese. Pour into a buttered casserole dish. Sprinkle parmesan cheese on top and bake for 30 minutes, uncovered at 375°F.

Spaghetti with Red Sauce

1 spaghetti squash
1/2 cup Classico Tomato Alfredo Sauce
1/4 cup Parmesan cheese

Makes 2 Servings	
Analysis per Serving:	
Carbs	**9.9g**
Calories	122.2
Fat	6.8g
Protein	6.5g

Preheat oven to 375°F

1. Slice the squash in half length wise and scoop out the seeds. Place face down on a buttered tray and bake for 30 minutes at 375°F. Cool for 5 minutes. Remove the insides carefully with a fork to maintain long strands.

2. Heat up pasta sauce. Pour over spaghetti squash, sprinkle parmesan cheese on top and serve.

Spinach Frittata

10 eggs
1/4 cup heavy cream
1 bunch spinach, chopped
1 glove garlic, crushed
1 Tbsp olive oil
2 Tbsp water
4 oz mushroom, canned, sliced
2 scallions, chopped
1/4 tsp salt & pepper, each
1/4 tsp nutmeg
1/4 tsp paprika
8 oz cream cheese
4 oz Romano cheese, grated

Makes 6 Servings	
Analysis per Serving:	
Carbs	**4.9g**
Calories	393.5
Fat	32.7g
Protein	20.3g

Set oven to 350°F.

1. Lightly sauté garlic in olive oil on medium heat. Add water and spinach, cover. Let steam for 1 minute. Drain on paper towels for just a minute.

2. Blend the cream cheese with the spinach while it's still warm so that the cheese melts. Mix in mushrooms and green onions.

3. Beat the eggs, cream, nutmeg and salt and pepper.

4. Using a lightly greased (olive oil is best) deep non-metallic pie dish, spread the spinach mixture evenly across bottom. Pour egg mixture over spinach. Sprinkle Romano cheese on top. Bake for 40 minutes. Cut into 6 pieces. Serve at once. Refrigerate left over.

Note:
Frozen chopped spinach works just as well. Completely thaw in microwave and drain well. Skip step 1 and add garlic with spinach.

Spinach Lasagna

16 oz ricotta cheese
3 lg. eggs
8 oz mozzarella cheese, sliced
1 package frozen chopped spinach, 10 oz
2 cloves garlic, crushed
2/3 cup Classico Tomato Alfredo Sauce
1/8 tsp cloves, ground
1 tsp Mrs. Dash, Garlic Blend

Makes 8 Servings	
Analysis per Serving:	
Carbs	**7.2g**
Calories	251.6
Fat	17.6g
Protein	17.2g

Set oven to 350°F

1. Defrost spinach in microwave. Drain well. Press several paper towels onto spinach to soak up a bit more liquid.

2. Beat eggs well. Add ricotta cheese, ground cloves, Mrs. Dash and spinach. Hand mix well.

3. Lightly grease a 8x8 non metallic baking dish with olive oil.

4. Place into baking dish 1/2 of the ricotta cheese mixture, spread evenly with a spatula. Drizzle about 1/3 cup of pasta sauce over the cheese. Sprinkle evenly 1/2 of the mozzarella cheese. Place remainder of ricotta cheese mixture, spread smooth. Pour remainder of pasta sauce and top with remainder of mozzarella.

5. Bake in 350°F oven for 30 minutes. Let cool for about 15 minutes prior to cutting and serving.

Note: Classico makes several red pasta sauces that range in carbs from 6g to 11g per 1/4 cup serving. This recipe has 6g carbs per 1/4 cup. Be careful of other brands of pasta sauce they are usually made with some sugar and have much higher carbs. Note that most white pasta sauces (e.g. Alfredo, four cheese sauce) are usually 2 or 3g carbs per 1/4 cup serving. You can use them in this recipe instead, although it's not as visually appealing as the red sauces.

Stir Fry Vegetables with Tofu

16 oz tofu, 2 firm cakes
 1 cup broccoli, chopped
 1 cup cauliflower, chopped
 1 cup Chinese cabbage, finely chopped
 1 bell pepper, chopped
 2 Tbsp sesame oil

Makes 6 Servings	
Analysis per Serving:	
Carbs	**6.8g**
Calories	130.6
Fat	9.1g
Protein	8.1g

Marinade:
 1/3 cup soy sauce
 1/2 cup water
 1/4 cup rice vinegar
 1/2 packet Sweet 'n Low® sweetener
1 1/2 tsp ground ginger
 1/4 tsp garlic powder
  1 tsp sesame oil
 1/4 tsp ground cloves

1. Wrap tofu cakes in double layer of dish towels or lots of paper towels. Press tofu by placing on top of them a cutting board weighted with several canned goods (about 3 pounds worth). Let set for 10 or more minutes. Cut tofu into bite sized cubes.

2. Mix well soy sauce, vinegar, oil, water, sweetener, ginger, garlic and clove.

3. Place tofu and vegetables in a non-metallic bowl. Pour in marinade and let marinate for 2 hours. If sauce does not completely cover tofu and veggies, be sure to lightly stir them after 1 hour. Drain before cooking. Reserve liquid.

4. Heat oil in large skillet. Add tofu, fry for 2-5 minutes per side. Add veggies and cook another 3-5 minutes or until desired tenderness. Add 1/2 or more of reserved liquid and heat for 1 minute. Serve.

Teriyaki Tofu

16 oz tofu, 2 firm cakes
  2 Tbsp butter

1/3 cup soy sauce
1/2 cup water
1/2 packet Sweet 'n Low® sweetener
  2 tsp ground ginger
1/4 tsp garlic powder
  1 tsp sesame oil
1/2 tsp mustard

Makes 4 Servings	
Analysis per Serving:	
Carbs	**4.9g**
Calories	163.0
Fat	12.3g
Protein	10.6g

1. Wrap tofu cakes in double layer of dish towels or lots of paper towels. Press tofu by placing on top of them a cutting board weighted with several canned goods (about 3 pounds worth). Let set for 10 or more minutes. Slice each tofu cake into 4 cutlets.

2. Mix well soy sauce, oil, water, sweetener, ginger, garlic and mustard.

3. Place tofu in a non-metallic baking pan. Pour teriyaki sauce over tofu and let marinate for 2 hours. If sauce does not completely cover tofu, be sure to turn them over after 1 hour. Place tofu on paper towel to drain for just a minute before cooking.

4. Melt butter in large skillet. Add tofu and fry for 2 or 3 minutes per side or until golden brown. Serve.

Tofu Italiano

16 oz tofu, 2 firm cakes
2 Tbsp butter
1 cup Italian salad dressing
1/2 cup Classico Tomato Alfredo Sauce
1/2 cup Parmesan cheese, grated

Makes 4 Servings	
Analysis per Serving:	
Carbs	**9.9g**
Calories	486.5
Fat	44.2g
Protein	14.8g

1. Wrap tofu cakes in double layer of dish towels or lots of paper towels. Press tofu by placing on top of them a cutting board weighted with several canned goods (about 3 pounds worth). Let set for 10 or more minutes. Slice each tofu cake into 4 cutlets.

2. Place tofu in a non-metallic baking pan. Pour Italian dressing over tofu and let marinate for 2 hours. If dressing does not completely cover tofu, be sure to turn them over after 1 hour. Place tofu on paper towel to drain for just a minute before cooking. Discard marinade.

3. Melt butter in large skillet. Add tofu and fry for 2 or 3 minutes per side or until golden brown.

4. Place tofu back into baking dish. Cover with pasta sauce and sprinkle the cheese on top. Bake until hot (approx. 10 minutes) in a 350°F oven. Serve.

Tofu Stuffed Peppers

16 oz tofu, 2 firm cakes
  6 green bell peppers
  2 Tbsp olive oil
  2 scallions, chopped
  2 garlic cloves, minced
1/2 cup mushrooms, chopped
2/3 cup cabbage, chopped fine
1/2 cup Classico Tomato Alfredo Sauce
1/2 cup parmesan cheese, grated

Makes 6 Servings	
Analysis per Serving:	
Carbs	**9.9g**
Calories	174.7
Fat	11.5g
Protein	2.7g

Set oven to 350°F

1. Wrap tofu cakes in double layer of dish towels or lots of paper towels. Press tofu by placing on top of them a cutting board weighted with several canned goods (about 3 pounds worth). Let set for 10 or more minutes. Crumble each tofu cake.

2. Heat olive oil in skillet. Add green onions, garlic, mushrooms and cabbage. Sauté, stirring frequently until cabbage has completely wilted.

3. Place sautéed vegetables in mixing bowl. Add tofu, pasta sauce and parmesan cheese. Toss well.

4. Cut off tops of bell peppers, remove stem and seeds. Loosely stuff peppers with tofu mixture. Place on cookie sheet and bake for 20 minutes at 350°F.

Zucchini Boats

2 zucchini
4 oz ricotta cheese
1 egg
2 Tbsp pesto sauce
1 Tbsp butter
1 garlic clove, crushed
1/4 tsp salt
1/4 tsp black pepper, coarsely ground
2 oz parmesan cheese, grated

Makes 4 Servings	
Analysis per Serving:	
Carbs	**4.3g**
Calories	206.2
Fat	15.6g
Protein	12.7g

Set oven to 350°F

1. Cut zucchini lengthwise. Scoop out seed portion, set aside. Place zucchini, cut side down, in a baking dish with a 1/4 inch of water. Bake at 350°F for 20 minutes.

2. Beat egg well. Add pesto, salt and pepper. Mix well.

3. Sauté garlic in butter for 1 minute. Add seed portion of zucchini and sauté another minute. Drain and mix with ricotta.

4. Scoop ricotta into zucchini halves, sprinkle on cheese. Bake at 350°F for 20 minutes. Serve.

Meats

MEATS

Baked Fresh Ham
Barbecued Spareribs
Beef and Mushrooms
Beef Fajitas
Beef Pot Roast
Beef Stroganoff
Beef Tenderloin Roll
Beef Tenderloin with Horseradish Sauce
Carne Asada
Corned Beef and Cabbage
Filet Mignon
Grilled Pork Chops with Chive Cream
Gypsy Style Steak
Ham Con Queso
Lamb Chops with Mint Glaze
Meat Balls
Meat Loaf
Mexican Plate
Mustard Coated Flank Steak
Pork Chop and Cabbage Casserole
Pork Chops with Orange Glaze
Pork Korma
Pork Roast
Prime Rib Roast
Shepherd's Pie
Shish Kebab
Spareribs & Sauerkraut
Steak Au Poivre
Stuffed Cabbage
Sweet & Sour Spareribs
Veal Marsala

Baked Fresh Ham

10 lbs fresh ham
2 garlic clove, minced
2 Tbsp olive oil
1/2 tsp dried rosemary
1/2 tsp ground thyme
1 cup chicken stock

Makes 10 Servings	
Analysis per Serving:	
Carbs	**0.4g**
Calories	231.2
Fat	14.6g
Protein	19.8g

Set oven to 350°F

1. Trim excess fat from ham.

2. Mix oil with herbs and rub all over ham. Bake at 350°F for 30-35 minutes per pound of meat, until meat thermometer registers 185°F. Baste occasionally with chicken stock.

Barbecued Spareribs

2 lb spareribs, country style
1/2 cup Lauri's barbecue sauce

Makes 2 Servings	
Analysis per Serving:	
Carbs	**6.0g**
Calories	1013.6
Fat	87.1g
Protein	48.9g

Preheat oven to 450°F.

1. Bake spareribs for 15 minutes at 450°F.

2. Reduce heat to 350°F, pour barbecue sauce over ribs and bake uncovered for 1 hour longer. Serve.

The last five minutes of baking can be under the broiler or on the grill.

Beef & Mushrooms

2 lbs ribeye steak
2 portobella mushrooms, sliced
2 scallions, chopped
1 garlic clove, crushed
1 Tbsp, butter
1 Tbsp, sherry
1/2 tsp Kitchen Bouquet
1/4 tsp salt & pepper, each

Makes 2 Servings	
Analysis per Serving:	
Carbs	**5.0g**
Calories	696.5
Fat	55.1g
Protein	41.4g

1. Cut way bone from steaks, then cut meat into strips. Thicker strips for medium rare and thinner strips for well done.

2. Melt butter and sauté garlic and mushrooms for 1 minute. Add sherry, Kitchen Bouquet, salt & pepper and steak strips and cook for 2 minutes, stirring occasionally.

3. Add scallions, stir for 30 seconds. Serve

Beef Fajitas

2 lbs steak, sliced
1 cup green bell pepper, sliced
1 cup red bell pepper, sliced
1 cup onion, sliced
2 Tbsp butter
2 Tbsp fajita seasoning
4 oz cheddar cheese, grated
4 Tbsp sour cream
4 Tbsp guacamole

Makes 4 Servings	
Analysis per Serving:	
Carbs	**8.7g**
Calories	553.6
Fat	45.0g
Protein	28.9g

1. In a large skillet, sauté pepper, onion and fajita seasoning in butter until tender. Remove from skillet and cook beef slices until cooked through.

2. Add peppers and onions, mix and heat through. Remove from heat.

3. Sprinkle cheese over meat, serve with sour cream and guacamole.

Note: I like "The Spice Hunter" fajita seasonings but there are quite a few other brands available.

Beef Pot Roast

1/4 cup red wine
2 cups beef bouillon
1 tsp salt
6 peppercorns
1 tsp allspice
1 packet Sweet 'n Low®, optional
1 bay leaf
1/2 onion, sliced
3 lbs beef pot roast
1/4 cup bacon fat (if roast does not have much fat on it)
1 stalk celery, sliced

Makes 6 Servings	
Analysis per Serving:	
Carbs	**6.9g**
Calories	396.0
Fat	30.1g
Protein	22.5g

1. Mix together wine, vinegar, bouillon, salt, peppercorns, allspice, sweetener, bay leaf, and sliced onion. Pour marinade over roast, turn to coat, and marinate at least two hours or over night, turning once or twice.

2. Remove roast from marinade and pat dry.

3. In heavy pan, sear meat quickly on all sides in smoking hot bacon fat. Pour off fat. Reduce heat low.

4. Add marinating liquid. Cover and simmer until tender, about 3-1/2 hours.

5. Add celery during last hour of cooking. When done, place roast on a platter and keep warm.

6. Strain liquids then reduce over medium-high heat until liquid measures about 2 cups. Season to taste. Serve liquids with sliced roast. (See "Brown Gravy" if you prefer).

Beef Stroganoff

2 lbs beef tenderloin, cut in thin strips
2 Tbsp butter
2 Tbsp olive oil
2 cups beef bouillon
1/4 cup sour cream
1/2 tsp paprika
1/4 tsp oregano
1/2 tsp Kitchen Bouquet
   salt & pepper to taste

Makes 4 Servings	
Analysis per Serving:	
Carbs	**2.1g**
Calories	474.3
Fat	41.9g
Protein	21.3g

1. Melt butter with oil and brown the beef (about 5 minutes). Slowly add bouillon to beef, stirring well. Bring to a boil.

2. Combine sour cream, paprika, oregano, Kitchen Bouquet and salt. Slowly stir sour cream mixture into beef mixture. Turn heat to low and bring to a bare simmer. Cook 15-20 minutes, stirring frequently and never allowing mixture to boil. Serve.

Beef Tenderloin Roll

3 lbs beef tenderloin, trimmed of fat
4 bacon strips, diced
1 bunch spinach, washed and dried
2 Tbsp Dijon mustard
2 Tbsp brandy
2 Tbsp olive oil

Makes 6 Servings	
Analysis per Serving:	
Carbs	0.7g
Calories	402.2
Fat	32.9g
Protein	21.9g

1. To make a flat 3/4-inch-thick piece of beef, butterfly tenderloin by cutting, from top to bottom, through center to within 3/4-inch of bottom; open like a book and press to flatten. Flatten tenderloin slightly with a meat pounder or side of a meat cleaver so that whole piece is about the same thickness.

2. In a large skillet over medium heat, sauté diced bacon until golden brown. When fat is rendered and bacon is crisp, pour off most of fat. Add spinach and cook until wilted (about 1-3 minutes). Remove from heat and cool for 1 minute.

3. Place spinach-bacon mixture over tenderloin. Spread evenly. Roll up tenderloin, jelly-roll fashion. Tie with kitchen twine in 4 places to fasten tightly.

4. In a small bowl mix together mustard and brandy. Rub over tenderloin. At this point, meat can be refrigerated for about 8 hours, if desired; but bring meat to room temperature 1 hour before cooking.

5. Preheat oven to 425°F.

6. Return skillet to medium heat, add olive oil, and place tenderloin, seam side down, in skillet; brown on all sides (5 minutes per side). Place tenderloin in oven; roast until medium-rare (about 40 minutes, or until internal temperature is 140°F on an instant-read thermometer). Let tenderloin rest 12 to 15 minutes, before slicing. Slice into 6 pieces and serve immediately.

Beef Tenderloin with Horseradish Sauce

4 lbs beef tenderloin
4 garlic clove, crushed
1 tsp salt
1 tsp black pepper
1 tsp thyme
1/4 tsp Tabasco sauce
1 cup soy sauce
1/2 cup red wine
1/2 cup olive oil
1 bay leaf
5 bacon strips

Makes 8 Servings	
Analysis per Serving:	
Carbs	**5.8g**
Calories	531.7
Fat	44.7g
Protein	24.0g

SAUCE
1/2 cup sour cream
2 Tbsp horseradish, to taste
1 Tbsp parsley, fresh, chopped
2 Tbsp scallions, minced
1 tsp lemon juice
   salt, to taste

1. Combine Tabasco, soy sauce, wine, oil, thyme, pepper, garlic and salt. Roll meat into mixture to cover all sides. Add bay leaf and marinate for at least 3 hours, turn occasionally.

2. Sauce: Mix together all sauce ingredients. Refrigerate several hours.

3. Remove meat for refrigerator 1 hour before cooking. Preheat oven to 425°F.

4. Place meat in a roasting pan and cover with bacon strips. Cook at 425°F for 10 minutes. Reduce heat to 350°F and continue to cook until meat thermometer reaches 160°F for medium (about 40 to 60 minutes). Let stand for 5 to 10 minutes. Slice diagonally. Serve with Horseradish sauce.

Carne Asada

4 steaks
2 Tbsp fresh lime juice
1/4 cup Colby cheese, shredded
1/4 cup Monterey Jack cheese, shredded
1/2 cup Lauri's Salsa de Cilantro
      or other low-carb salsa

Makes 4 Servings	
Analysis per Serving:	
Carbs	**2.0g**
Calories	751.9
Fat	62.7g
Protein	43.7g

1. Place steaks in utility dish; pierce with fork. Sprinkle both sides of steaks with lime juice, rubbing into surface. Cover and refrigerate while preparing coals.

2. Place steaks on grill over medium coals. Grill steaks 7 to 9 minutes for rare to medium, turning once.

3. Trim excess fat from steaks; carve steaks into slices.

4. Toss meat with cheese. Serve with salsa.

Corned Beef & Cabbage

5 lb beef brisket
3 whole cloves
1/4 onion
1/4 cup bell pepper
3 garlic clove
1/2 cup rosemary
1 cup celery
3 sprigs parsley
6 black peppercorns
2 bay leaves
1 head cabbage

Makes 8 Servings	
Analysis per Serving:	
Carbs	**6.1g**
Calories	471.8
Fat	37.9g
Protein	25.6g

1. Place beef in a large pot, cover with cold water and bring to a boil.

2. To form garni, place onion, cloves, garlic, peppers, celery, rosemary, parsley, peppercorns and bay leaves in a cloth and tie with a string.

3. When beef comes to a boil, drain and add fresh water with the garni bag and bring to a boil. Reduce heat to a simmer for approximately 5 hours.

4. During last 30 minutes of cooking, add cabbage in wedges. Serve with mustard.

Filet Mignon

2 filet mignon
2 bacon strips
2 Tbsp hollandaise sauce

Makes 2 Servings	
Analysis per Serving:	
Carbs	**0.3g**
Calories	754.6
Fat	64.1g
Protein	46.4g

Wrap bacon around each fillet and secure with tooth picks. Grill for 4 minutes per side (medium rare). Remove from grill, top with hollandaise sauce and serve.

Grilled Pork Chops with Chive Cream

2 Tbsp vegetable oil
1 tsp salt
1/2 tsp ground white pepper
1 shallots, crushed
3 lbs pork chops (4 large chops)

Makes 4 Servings	
Analysis per Serving:	
Carbs	**3.1g**
Calories	634.9
Fat	56.6g
Protein	55.0g

Chive Cream:
1 cup whipping cream
1/4 tsp lemon extract
1/4 tsp salt
1/8 tsp ground white pepper
1/4 cup minced fresh chives

1. In a shallow pan, stir together oil, salt, pepper, and shallots. Place pork chops in pan, coat with marinade on both sides, and let rest for 15 to 30 minutes.

2. Chive Cream: In a small saucepan over medium heat, place cream and lemon extract. Simmer until reduced by about one third; keep warm over low heat. Just before serving, season with salt and pepper, then stir chives into warm cream sauce.

3. Prepare a charcoal fire or preheat broiler. Place pork chops on grill or under broiler, about 4 inches from heat, and cook until browned on one side (about 4 minutes). Turn and cook second side until lightly browned and slightly firm. Serve chops immediately, drizzled with Chive Cream.

This recipes is also great with veal chops instead of the pork.

Gypsy Style Steak

2 Tbsp butter
1 Tbsp salad oil
1/4 onion, finely chopped
1/2 sweet red pepper, seeded and chopped
1/4 lb mushrooms, sliced
1 garlic clove, minced
4 boneless steaks (blade-cut chuck roast)
   dash salt
   dash paprika
1/4 cup dry white wine
1/2 cup sour cream
1 Tbsp parsley, chopped

Makes 4 Servings	
Analysis per Serving:	
Carbs	**4.5g**
Calories	808.7
Fat	67.5g
Protein	42.2g

1. In a large frying pan, heat 1 Tbsp of the butter and salad oil. Cook onion, red pepper, mushrooms, and garlic, stirring frequently, until tender; remove vegetable mixture from the pan.

2. Sprinkle steaks with salt and paprika. Add remaining butter to pan in which vegetables were cooked. Brown steaks on both sides over high heat (about 4 minutes per side). Remove to a warm serving platter.

3. Add wine to pan and cook quickly to reduce slightly, stirring to loosen browned juices from pan. Reduce heat to moderate, mix in vegetables, and cook until heated through. Over low heat, smoothly mix in sour cream (do not boil). Serve immediately. Spoon sauce over steaks. Sprinkle with parsley.

Ham Con Queso

1 lb cooked ham, cubed
1/4 cup onion, chopped
1 cup cheese sauce mexicana (see Sauces)
1 Tbsp butter
1 Tbsp parsley, chopped

Makes 2 Servings	
Analysis per Serving:	
Carbs	**2.9g**
Calories	692.7
Fat	49.6g
Protein	50.3g

1. Sauté onions in butter until translucent. Pour off excess butter.

2. Add ham cubes cook until warmed through and turning brown. Add cheese sauce and parsley, heat just enough to warm it. Serve.

Goes well with cauliflower.

Note: Check the labels on your ham; some have honey or sugar added; don't buy them. There are many brands that have 0g carbs.

Lamb Chops with Mint Glaze

4 Lamb chops
4 Tbsp butter
1 packet Sweet 'n Low®
1/2 tsp mint extract

Makes 4 Servings	
Analysis per Serving:	
Carbs	**0.2g**
Calories	457.9
Fat	42.0g
Protein	18.9g

1. Grill lamb chops.

2. Melt butter, add sweetener and mint extract. Pour over chops.

Meat Balls

1.5 lbs ground beef
1 lbs ground pork
3 eggs
1/2 tsp garlic salt
1/2 tsp black pepper
1/2 tsp thyme
1/4 tsp sage, ground
1 Tbsp Worcestershire sauce

2 Tbsp butter
cooking oil
1 cup Classico Tomato Alfredo Sauce

Makes 4 Servings	
Analysis per Serving:	
Carbs	**7.0g**
Calories	600.3
Fat	47.3g
Protein	35.5g

1. Beat eggs. Add seasonings and Worcestershire sauce. Beat well.

2. Add meat and blend well with hands. Form meat balls by rolling a portion in the palm of your hands (rubbing a little oil on your hands helps the meat from sticking). The smaller the meat balls the faster they cook.

3. Heat ¼ of the butter and enough oil to cover the bottom of a large skillet on medium high heat. Add ¼ of the meat balls and brown all around. Remove with a slotted spoon to platter and keep warm in a oven. Repeat until all the meat balls are cooked.

4. Pour off liquids and add pasta sauce. Heat through then pour over meat balls.

5. If meat balls are large and you doubt if they are cooked all through then bake in a 350°F oven for 15 or 20 minutes before serving. Serve warm.

Notes:
1. Meat balls with no sauce, has less than 1g carb each.
2. Try serving over spaghetti squash (adds 1.7g carbs per serving if 1 whole squash is used for a serving for 4 people).

Meat Loaf

1.5 lbs ground beef
1.5 lbs ground pork
 3 eggs
1/2 tsp garlic salt
1/4 tsp black pepper
1/4 tsp thyme
1/4 tsp sage, ground
 1 Tbsp Worcestershire sauce
 1 Tbsp sherry
1/2 cup scallions, minced
 5 oz sharp cheddar cheese, grated

Makes 6 Servings	
Analysis per Serving:	
Carbs	**1.8g**
Calories	484.1
Fat	37.2g
Protein	33.2g

Set oven to 375°F

1. Beat eggs. Add seasonings, Worcestershire sauce and sherry. Beat well.

2. Add meats and blend well with hands. Add scallions and cheese. Blend well.

3. Place in an oiled meat loaf pan and bake at 375°F for 45 minutes. Let cool for 5 minutes before slicing and serving.

Mexican Plate

2 lbs ground beef
2 package taco seasoning mix (Taco Bell's)
1/4 cup water
6 oz shredded cheddar cheese
4 Tbsp scallions, chopped
4 Tbsp sour cream
8 Tbsp salsa

Makes 4 Servings	
Analysis per Serving:	
Carbs	**7.5g**
Calories	576.2
Fat	48.7g
Protein	26.1g

1. Crumble ground beef into a ceramic bowl. Microwave on high for 3 to 6 minutes, just until meat is no longer pink when stirred. Drain. Add taco seasoning and 1/4 cup of water. Stir. Microwave for 2 more minutes.

2. Divide meat onto 4 individual serving plates. Sprinkle 1/4 of the cheese over each plate. Sprinkle scallions over each plate.

3. Return each plate to microwave for 30 seconds or until cheese melts.

4. Garnish each plate with 1 tablespoon sour cream and 2 tablespoons salsa. Serve immediately.

Note: Be sure to check the label on the salsa, not all are low carb.

Mustard Coated Flank Steak

1/2 cup Dijon mustard
1/4 cup soy sauce
  2 Tbsp heavy cream
  2 tsp crumbled thyme
  2 tsp fresh ginger root, peeled & minced
1/2 tsp cracked black peppercorns
  3 lbs flank steak

Makes 6 Servings	
Analysis per Serving:	
Carbs	**6.7g**
Calories	440.4
Fat	38.4g
Protein	18.3g

1. Mix all ingredients except beef in a small bowl.

2. Put steaks on a large plate or lasagna dish. Pour mustard sauce over steak and marinate covered for at least 6 hours or overnight, in refrigerator.

3. Cook over hot grill for about 6 minutes for each side (for medium rare).

4. Transfer to cutting board. Cut steaks diagonally across grain into 1/4 to 3/8 inch thick slices.

You can heat the marinate and pour over slices before serving.

Pork Chop & Cabbage Casserole

1/2 green cabbage
  1 cup heavy cream
    salt & pepper
  4 pork chops, well trimmed
  2 Tbsp butter
1/4 cup white wine
  1 pinch sage
3/4 cup grated Parmesan cheese

Makes 4 Servings	
Analysis per Serving:	
Carbs	**8.6g**
Calories	678.1
Fat	52.5g
Protein	40.4g

1. Remove the outside leaves of a small young cabbage, slice it fine, and boil it for 7 minutes in salted water. Drain the cabbage thoroughly, add salt and pepper and 1 cup of cream, and simmer it, covered, for 30 minutes.

2. Meanwhile, in a covered iron skillet, sauté 4 well-trimmed pork chops in butter for 20 minutes, or until they are brown. Turn at least once. Remove the chops and season them with salt and freshly ground pepper.

3. Stir white wine briskly into the pan juices, add a good pinch of sage, and simmer the mixture for a couple of minutes. Stir this juice into the creamed cabbage.

4. Spread half the cabbage in the bottom of an oven-proof casserole. Add the pork chops, cover them with the rest of the cabbage, sprinkle with grated Parmesan and a little melted butter.

5. Bake the casserole, uncovered , in a 350°F oven for 20 minutes, or until the top is golden brown.

Pork Chops with Orange Glaze

4 Pork chops
4 Tbsp butter
1 packet Sweet 'n Low®
1/2 tsp orange extract

Makes 4 Servings	
Analysis per Serving:	
Carbs	**0.2g**
Calories	399.0
Fat	30.2g
Protein	29.7g

1. Grill pork chops (approx. 5 minutes per side).

2. Melt butter, add sweetener and orange extract. Pour over pork chops.

Pork Korma

2 lbs pork tenderloin, cubed
4 Tbsp ghee (or butter)
1 Tbsp ginger root, peeled and grated
2 garlic clove, crushed
2 scallions, chopped
1/4 tsp chili powder
2 Tbsp ground coriander
1/2 cup sour cream
2 cups heavy cream
1/2 tsp cinnamon
1/2 tsp cardamom
1/4 tsp mace

Makes 4 Servings	
Analysis per Serving:	
Carbs	**7.2g**
Calories	641.2
Fat	57.0g
Protein	27.3g

1. Melt ghee on medium heat and sauté onions, garlic and ginger for 1 minute. Add coriander and chili powder and sauté 1 more minute.

2. Increase heat and add pork, stir occasionally until browned.

3. Reduce heat to medium. Add about 1/4 of sour cream, stir until juices reduce, repeat until all of sour cream is reduced. Add heavy cream, cinnamon, cardamom and mace. Bring just to a boil, reduce heat and simmer 30 minutes. Serve.

MEATS

Pork Roast

	Makes 4 Servings	
2 lbs pork loin roast	**Makes 4 Servings**	
1 garlic clove	Analysis per Serving:	
1 Tbsp olive oil	**Carbs**	**1.6g**
1/8 tsp each of sage, rosemary & thyme	Calories	334.1
1/2 cup heavy cream	Fat	24.1g
2 egg yolk	Protein	27.0g
1/2 tsp Kitchen Bouquet		

Remove roast from refrigerator at least 1 hour before cooking.
Set oven to 325°F.

1. Rinse and pat dry the roast. Rub pork roast with garlic. Pour oil and herbs (including left over garlic) into roasting dish. Roll roast in oil/herb mixture until well covered.

2. Roast, uncovered, with fat side up for 1 hour & 10 minutes (35 minutes to the pound) or until internal temperature reaches 170°F (185°F for shoulder cut). Remove from oven and let sit 10 minutes before carving.

3. To make sauce: Beat egg yolk with the cream. Slowly add to pan drippings over medium heat, stirring constantly. Add Kitchen Bouquet and salt & pepper to taste. (See "Brown Gravy" as an alternative.)

4. Carve roast and drizzle a little sauce over each slice. Serve.

Prime Rib Roast

6 lbs prime rib roast
   salt
   fresh ground black pepper
1/2 tsp dried rosemary

Makes 6 Servings	
Analysis per Serving:	
Carbs	**0.1g**
Calories	1352.1
Fat	113.9g
Protein	76.2g

Heat oven to 500°F.

1. Put the rib roast in roasting pan, season with salt and pepper and rosemary, and sear in preheated oven for 15 minutes. Lower heat to 350°F. and cook until internal temperature reaches 130°F, about 1 1/4 hours, for medium-rare. Remove roast from oven, cover with a sheet of foil, and let rest for about 10 minutes.

2. Put roast with ribs down on a cutting board and cut into thick or thin slices. For thin slices, cut meat off the ribs. For thick ones, cut between the ribs as necessary.

Shepherd's Pie

2 cups leftover Lauri's beef stew
2 cups Lauri's mock mashed potatoes

Makes 2 Servings	
Analysis per Serving:	
Carbs	**7.8g**
Calories	414.3
Fat	32.1g
Protein	19.2g

Set oven to 350°F

1. Divide your left over beef or lamb stew into two individual serving dishes.

2. Careful top with mock mashed potatoes (creamed cauliflower). Heat in oven at 350°F until slightly browned. Serve.

Shish Kebabs

2 lbs beef or lamb stew meat,
    cut into 2" chunks
1/4 cup olive oil
1/4 cup red wine
1/4 tsp lemon extract
  1 clove garlic, minced
  2 tsp ginger root, minced very fine
  1 tsp onion salt
1/2 tsp black pepper
1/4 tsp cayenne pepper
  1 tsp curry powder
  1 tsp turmeric
  1 tsp coriander ground

1/2 red onion, sliced into squares
  1 sweet green peppers, seeded and slice into squares
  1 red or yellow bell peppers, seeded and slice into squares
12 large, mushrooms
  6 skewers

Makes 6 Servings	
Analysis per Serving:	
Carbs	**8.2g**
Calories	229.3
Fat	14.4g
Protein	13.7g

1. Blend olive oil with wine and lemon extract. Stir in ginger, garlic, and spices. Place meat chunks in marinade and turn to coat. Marinate overnight, turning pieces occasionally.

2. Thread meat and vegetables onto skewers. Grill over hot coals until everything is well browned (usually 3 minutes per side).

Spareribs & Sauerkraut

1/2 yellow onions, sliced
12 oz sauerkraut (unsweetened)
 2 lbs spareribs

Makes 4 Servings	
Analysis per Serving:	
Carbs	**6.5g**
Calories	422.3
Fat	34.1g
Protein	24.8g

Set oven to 500°F

Place onions in casserole dish. Spread sauerkraut over onions. Place ribs on top. Brown in a 500°F oven for 15 minutes, reduce heat to 350°F, cover tightly, and bake 1 hour.

Steak Au Poivre

 2 steaks, 1" thick
 1 Tbsp black pepper, coarsely ground
 3 Tbsp sherry
 1 Tbsp butter
1/2 tsp Kitchen Bouquet
 1 tsp arrowroot
 1 Tbsp water
    salt, to taste

Makes 2 Servings	
Analysis per Serving:	
Carbs	**7.2g**
Calories	741.6
Fat	55.0g
Protein	40.7g

1. Firmly press pepper into steaks. Pour sherry onto a plate. Dredge steaks through sherry. (Reserve sherry).

2. Grill steaks 3 minutes per side for medium rare.

3. Sauce: Melt butter over medium heat. Add sherry (hopefully some of the pepper fell in) and Kitchen Bouquet. Mix water and arrowroot thoroughly. While mixing, pour into sauce. Stir constantly until sauce has thicken. Add salt if needed.

4. Pour sauce over grilled steak and serve.

Stuffed Cabbage

12 large cabbage leaves
1 lb ground beef
1/2 lb sausage meat
1 egg, beaten
1/2 tsp salt
1/4 tsp black pepper
1/2 tsp thyme
1/4 tsp allspice
8 oz sauerkraut
2 Tbsp onion, finely chopped

Makes 6 Servings	
Analysis per Serving:	
Carbs	**9.4g**
Calories	440.8
Fat	36.8g
Protein	19.5g

Set oven to 350°F

1. Remove twelve large leaves from cabbage. Blanch one minute and drain.

2. Mix ground beef, sausage, salt, pepper, thyme, allspice, sauerkraut and onion.

3. Divide into twelve parts and shape each into a log two inches shorter than a cabbage leaf. Place one meat log lengthwise on each cabbage leaf. Fold one side over meat, then fold ends over, and finally fold remaining side. Place, seam side down, in a single layer in large, shallow baking dish.

4. Bake at 350°F for 1 to 1-1/2 hours, until meat is cooked through.

Sweet & Sour Spareribs

2 lb spareribs, country style
1/3 cup vinegar
2 Tbsp soy sauce
1 Tbsp sherry
2 tsp fresh ginger root, grated
1 pkg Sweet 'n Low® sweetener

Makes 2 Servings	
Analysis per Serving:	
Carbs	**5.2g**
Calories	833.9
Fat	66.5g
Protein	49.1g

Preheat oven to 350°F.

1. Parboil spareribs for 3 minutes.

2. Mix remaining ingredients together.

3. Place spareribs in casserole dish, cover with sauce. Bake for 1 hour, basting occasionally. Serve.

Veal Marsala

1 lb veal
2/3 cup Parmesan cheese
1/2 tsp ground oregano
1/4 tsp ground sage
1/4 tsp garlic salt
1/4 tsp black pepper

2 Tbsp olive oil
6 oz mushrooms, sliced
1 cup water
1/3 cup Marsala wine
1 beef bouillon cube
1/4 tsp ground red pepper
1/4 cup parsley, chopped

Makes 2 Servings	
Analysis per Serving:	
Carbs	**7.3g**
Calories	524.3
Fat	32.7g
Protein	43.7g

1. Place veal pieces between 2 sheets of heavy duty plastic wrap. Flatten to 1/4 inch thickness with mallet or rolling pin. Cut large pieces in two.

2. Combine 1/3 cup of Parmesan cheese with oregano, sage, garlic salt and pepper. Dredge veal. Press cheese mixture into veal if it will not stick.

3. Heat 1 tablespoon of the oil in large skillet on medium/high heat. Cook veal 1 minute per side or until slightly browned. Remove, keep warm. Repeat with oil and veal until all veal pieces are cooked.

4. Add to the skillet mushrooms, water, Marsala wine, bouillon and red pepper. Bring to a boil & cook for 6 minutes or until reduced to about 1 cup. Stir frequently.

5. Reduce heat to medium. Return veal to the skillet, turning to coat and cook for about 2 minutes until heated completely. Serve with remaining Parmesan cheese and chopped parsley garnish.

Poultry

POULTRY

Alfredo Chicken
Almond Chicken
Baked Cornish Game Hens
Chicken & Broccoli Au Gratin
Chicken Cacciatore
Chicken Cordon Bleu
Chicken Divan
Chicken Fajitas
Chicken Florentine
Chicken Italiano
Chicken with Peanut Sauce
Chicken with Smoked Mozzarella and Pesto
Creamy Smoked Chicken
Curried Chicken
Curried Turkey
Jerk Chicken
Mediterranean Chicken
Oriental Grilled Chicken
Roast Duckling with Sherry
Turkey Mushroom Melt

Alfredo Chicken

4 chicken breast, boneless
4 chicken thighs, boneless
4 garlic cloves, sliced
2 Tbsp butter
2 cups Alfredo Sauce
1 scallion, minced
8 oz Romano cheese, grated

Makes 4 Servings	
Analysis per Serving:	
Carbs	**6.4g**
Calories	1331.3
Fat	86.8g
Protein	120.6g

1. Chicken parts can be left whole or cut into bite sized pieces.

2. In large heavy skillet, heat butter and 1/2 of the garlic on medium high heat for 30 seconds. Add chicken, cover and cook for 6 minutes. Turn over each piece of chicken, cover and cook an additional 6 minutes. (If all the chicken does not fit well into your skillet then you can cook them in two batches.)

   Step 2 above is for whole pieces. If using bite size pieces, change step 2 to "cook chicken for 5 minutes, stirring frequently". If using pre-cooked chicken or turkey, skip step 2 & 3, reduce crushed garlic in half and add it to the casserole dish uncooked.

3. Remove chicken and place on paper towels for a few minutes to drain.

4. Smear remainder of garlic in a casserole dish large enough so that the chicken pieces will lay flat. Add the chicken. Evenly pour the Alfredo sauce over the chicken (smooth with spatula if needed).

5. Sprinkle chopped green onions over the chicken, then sprinkle the Romano cheese on top.

6. Bake in 350°F oven for 30 minutes. Let cool for about 5 minutes before serving.

Almond Chicken

4 whole skinless boneless chicken breasts
2 Tbsp soy sauce
1 Tbsp rice wine
1 packet Sweet 'n Low®
2 Tbsp chicken stock
1 inch ginger root, peeled & minced
1 garlic cloves, minced
1 egg
1/2 cup almonds, ground
6 cups peanut oil for frying

Makes 4 Servings	
Analysis per Serving:	
Carbs	**5.7g**
Calories	1483.7
Fat	147.3g
Protein	35.5g

1. Pat chicken dry with paper towels. Cut into strips 1/2" wide by 3" long.

2. Stir soy sauce, rice wine, chicken stock, sweetener, ginger, and garlic together. Place chicken in marinade, turning to coat. Marinate at least one hour, turning chicken after half an hour.

3. Remove chicken from marinade and drain on paper towels.

4. Beat egg slightly with 1/2 tsp water. One by one, dip chicken pieces in egg and roll in almonds to coat. Let almond coated pieces set 15 minutes.

5. Heat oil to 350°F. Fry chicken pieces in batches one layer deep until crisp, golden brown. Be sure to let oil come back up to 350°F between batches. Drain on paper towels and serve at once.

Baked Cornish Game Hens

6 whole Cornish game hens
1/2 medium onion, chopped
3 celery ribs, chopped
1/2 green peppers, chopped
10 oz mushrooms, chopped
1 garlic clove, minced
2 Tbsp fresh basil, minced
1 tsp oregano
2 Tbsp fresh parsley
3/4 cup butter, melted

Makes 6 Servings	
Analysis per Serving:	
Carbs	**4.7g**
Calories	1019.2
Fat	125.2g
Protein	106.8g

Set oven to 325°F

1. Stir 1/2 cup melted butter with onion, celery, green pepper, mushrooms, garlic, and herbs. Let cool.

2. Season hens inside and out with salt and pepper.

3. Stuff bird with equal amounts of the vegetable mix. Place birds in baking dish, breast side up. Drizzle with remaining 1/4 cup butter. Cover and bake 1-1/2 hours at 325°F. Brown at 500°F for 1 or 2 minutes. Serve.

Chicken & Broccoli Au Gratin

1 chicken, roasted
    (or left over chicken or turkey)
1 head broccoli
4 oz cheddar cheese
2 Tbsp soy sauce
1/2 tsp black pepper
1/4 tsp garlic salt

Makes 3 Servings	
Analysis per Serving:	
Carbs	**2.5g**
Calories	248.7
Fat	14.8g
Protein	25.4g

Set oven to 350°F

1. Remove meat from bones. Place meat in casserole dish.

2. Cut up broccoli into bite sized pieces. Steam for 2-3 minutes.

3. Mix soy sauce with seasoning. Toss with chicken and broccoli.

4. Place in casserole dish, cover with cheese and cook in 350°F oven until cheese is completely melted (10 to 15 minutes). Serve.

Chicken Cacciatore

3 lb whole chicken
 salt
 black pepper
 cayenne pepper
1/4 cup olive oil
1/2 medium onion, sliced thinly
 1 clove garlic, minced
1/2 large bell pepper, sliced thinly
 2 Italian plum tomatoes, coarsely chopped
1/4 tsp dried basil
1/4 tsp oregano
1/4 tsp rosemary
 4 oz mushrooms, sliced

Makes 3 Servings	
Analysis per Serving:	
Carbs	**7.3g**
Calories	282.6
Fat	20.6g
Protein	16.4g

1. Cut chicken into serving-size pieces. Season with salt, pepper, and cayenne.

2. In a Dutch oven or similar heavy kettle, sauté onions, garlic, and bell pepper in olive oil until limp. Remove from pan.

3. Brown chicken in same olive oil.

4. Add cooked onion mixture and remaining ingredients to kettle. Simmer over medium low heat until chicken is cooked through, ~30minutes.

Chicken Cordon Bleu

2 whole chicken breasts, boned and skinned
1/2 cup cooked ham, minced
1/2 cup cheddar cheese, grated
   salt
   black pepper
1 egg
4 cups peanut oil, for frying

Makes 2 Servings	
Analysis per Serving:	
Carbs	**0.7g**
Calories	1522.0
Fat	91.1g
Protein	90.9g

1. One at a time, place breast halves between two sheets of waxed paper and pound flat.

2. Combine minced ham and grated cheese with hands. Form into four rolls to fit in middle of a flattened breast half (about 3 inches long). Place a roll on each breast half and roll chicken around ham & cheese, secure with a tooth pick. Alternately, you can fold breast half around ham & cheese, beginning with one long side, then short sides, finishing with a long side -- like an envelope.

3. Beat egg lightly with 1 tsp water. Paint each chicken roll with egg mixture.

4. Heat peanut oil in a fryer or wok to 350°F. Fry chicken pieces, two at a time, in hot oil, until browned evenly and firm to the touch. Serve.

Chicken Divan

1 cup chicken broth
1/2 cup heavy cream
2/3 cup mayonnaise
3 Tbsp sherry
salt
black pepper
10 oz frozen broccoli, cooked
2 whole chickens, cooked , de-boned
1/4 cup Parmesan cheese

Makes 6 Servings	
Analysis per Serving:	
Carbs	**3.6g**
Calories	339.6
Fat	27.6g
Protein	21.0g

Set oven to 350°F

1. Mix well over low heat, broth, cream, mayonnaise, sherry, salt, and pepper.

2. Drain cooked broccoli and place in baking dish.

3. Pour half of the sherry sauce over the broccoli. Arrange slices of chicken on top. Pour remaining sauce over chicken and sprinkle with cheese. Bake at 350°F for 15-20 minutes.

Chicken Fajitas

2 lbs chicken breasts
1 cup green bell pepper, sliced
1 cup red bell pepper, sliced
1 cup onion, sliced
2 Tbsp butter
2 Tbsp fajita seasoning
4 oz cheddar cheese, grated

Makes 4 Servings	
Analysis per Serving:	
Carbs	**7.0g**
Calories	270.0
Fat	16.1g
Protein	24.2g

1. Cut chicken breasts into long thin slices.

2. In a large skillet, sauté pepper, onion and fajita seasoning in butter until tender. Remove from skillet.

3. In same skillet, cook chicken slices until cooked through (about 3 to 5 minutes). Add peppers and onions mix, to reheat. Remove from heat.

4. Place on serving platter. Sprinkle cheese over meat, serve with sour cream and guacamole.

Note: I like "The Spice Hunter" fajita seasonings but there are quite a few other brands available.

Chicken Florentine

1/2 lb fresh spinach, stems removed, washed
4 Tbsp butter
3 scallions, chopped
6 chicken breasts, cut into 2" pieces
6 oz mushrooms, sliced
1 Tbsp dry white wine
1 cup sour cream
1/4 tsp garlic salt
1/4 tsp nutmeg
4 oz Swiss cheese, grated

Makes 6 Servings	
Analysis per Serving:	
Carbs	5.7g
Calories	394.8
Fat	22.9g
Protein	40.8g

Set oven to 350°F

1. Steam chopped spinach until wilted, drain. Place in buttered casserole dish.

2. Melt 2 Tbsp of butter in large skillet and sauté onions until golden. Remove onions with slotted spoon, mix in with spinach.

3. Add 1 Tbsp butter to skillet. Brown chicken and remove to warm plate. Sauté mushrooms in remaining butter and remove to plate with chicken.

4. Add wine to pan and slowly add sour cream and stir until hot. Add chicken, mushrooms, and garlic powder. Stir and heat through. Pour onto spinach, top with Swiss cheese and bake uncovered at 350°F for 20 to 30 minutes.

Chicken Italiano

4 chicken breast, boneless
4 chicken thighs, boneless
4 garlic cloves, sliced
2 Tbsp butter
1 cup Classico Tomato Alfredo Sauce
6 oz Parmesan cheese, grated

Makes 4 Servings	
Analysis per Serving:	
Carbs	**8.1g**
Calories	659.9
Fat	45.3g
Protein	22.0g

Set oven to 350°F

1. Chicken parts can be left whole or cut into bite sized piece

   Step 2 below is for whole pieces. If using bite size pieces, change step 2 to "cook chicken for 5 minutes, stirring frequently". If using pre-cooked chicken or turkey, skip step 2, reduce crushed garlic in half and add it to the casserole dish uncooked.

2. In large heavy skillet, heat butter and1/2 of the garlic on medium high heat for 30 seconds. Add chicken, cover and cook for 6 minutes. Turn over each piece of chicken, cover and cook an additional 6 minutes. (If all the chicken does not fit well into your skillet then you can cook them in two batches.)

3. Remove chicken and place on paper towels for a few minutes to drain.

4. Smear remainder of garlic in a casserole dish large enough so that the chicken pieces will lay flat. Add the chicken. Evenly pour the pasta sauce over the chicken (smooth with spatula if needed).

5. Sprinkle the parmesan cheese on top. Bake in 350°F oven for 30 minutes. Let cool for about 5 minutes before serving.

Chicken with Spicy Peanut Sauce

1 roasted chicken, de-boned
1 Tbsp oil, peanut or sesame
2 scallions, chopped
2 garlic cloves, minced
1 tsp chili powder, optional
3 Tbsp peanut butter, chunky
3 Tbsp water
1 Tbsp soy sauce
1 tsp lime or lemon juice
1 packet Sweet 'n Low® sweetener
  salt and pepper, to taste

Makes 3 Servings	
Analysis per Serving:	
Carbs	**6.5g**
Calories	230.2
Fat	14.9g
Protein	19.1g

1. Cut chicken meat into bite sized pieces.

2. Heat oil on medium heat in skillet. Sauté scallions, garlic and chili powder for 1 minute. Remove from skillet (leaving as much oil as possible.

3. Turn up heat and brown chicken pieces until approximately half cooked. Remove from skillet.

4. Turn heat down to medium. Add peanut butter, water, soy sauce, lime juice and sweetener. Mix well. Add more water if sauce is too thick. Add salt & pepper to taste.

5. Add chicken, scallions and garlic back to skillet. Stir to coat chicken. Cook on medium heat for 5 to 10 minutes until chicken is cooked through. Serve.

Chicken with Mozzarella & Pesto

Pesto:
1/2 cup fresh basil leaves
1 Tbsp pine nuts
1 Tbsp grated Parmesan cheese
1 clove garlic
1/4 cup olive oil

4 boned and skinned chicken breasts
4 slices smoked mozzarella, 1/4-inch slices
2 Tbsp oil
1 Tbsp butter

1. For the pesto, combine the basil, pine nuts, Parmesan cheese, and garlic in a food processor and process until minced. With the machine running, slowly add olive oil, up to 1/4 cup, to form a paste.

   Pesto can be made several days ahead.

2. Make a pocket in each chicken breast by cutting horizontally into the side. Make each incision about 3/4 the length of the breast.

3. Fill pockets with the pesto and mozzarella and trim any cheese that is not totally enclosed.

   Recipe can be made to this point 1 day ahead.

4. Heat oil and butter in a frying pan over medium-high heat. Sauté chicken in butter and oil for about 5 minutes. Turn the chicken, lower heat to medium-low and continue cooking until cooked through, about 4 minutes. Serve immediately.

Creamy Smoked Chicken

8 boneless chicken breasts
2 packages chipped beef
8 bacon slices, uncooked
1 pint sour cream
1 can cream of mushroom soup
1/2 tsp paprika
1/2 tsp liquid Barbecue Smoke®

Set oven to 350°F

1. Line large baking dish with chipped beef.

2. Wrap bacon around each chicken breast; place in baking dish.

3. Mix sour cream, soup and liquid smoke; pour over chicken. Sprinkle paprika on top and cover with foil. Bake at 350°F for 1 hour.

Curried Chicken

1 roasted chicken, de-boned
1 cup onion, chopped
1 can coconut milk, unsweetened
1 packet Sweet 'n Low®
1 Tbsp ghee
2 tsp ginger, grated
1 Tbsp coriander seed, ground
1 tsp cumin, ground
1/2 tsp black pepper
1/2 tsp salt
1/4 tsp chili powder
1/2 tsp turmeric
1/4 tsp clove, ground
1 tsp lime juice
1 bunch cilantro, chopped

Makes 3 Servings	
Analysis per Serving:	
Carbs	**1.8g**
Calories	197.7
Fat	10.5g
Protein	16.3g

1. Cut up chicken into bite sized pieces.

2. Mix dried seasoning together.

3. In large skillet over medium high heat, sauté in ghee the seasoning and onion for 1 minute. Add lime juice and ginger, cook while stirring for 1 minute.

4. Add chicken, cook, stirring frequently for 5 minutes.

5. Add coconut milk, sweetener and cilantro; reduce heat to medium low. Cook for 15 minutes (do not boil). Serve.

Curried Turkey

2 lbs turkey breasts, skinned
1/2 tsp ground coriander
1/2 tsp paprika
1/4 tsp turmeric
1/2 tsp cumin
1/4 tsp cayenne pepper
1/4 tsp cinnamon
2 Tbsp grated ginger root
1 Tbsp olive oil
1/4 tsp lemon extract
1/2 cup sour cream
2 minced green onions, for garnish

Makes 4 Servings	
Analysis per Serving:	
Carbs	**4.4g**
Calories	423.9
Fat	22.7g
Protein	49.1g

1. Place turkey breasts in a large baking pan.

2. In a small bowl combine coriander, paprika, turmeric, cumin, cayenne, cinnamon, ginger root, olive oil, lemon extract, and sour cream. Spread over top of turkey breasts. Cover pan with plastic wrap and refrigerate for 2 hours.

3. Preheat oven to 350°F. Unwrap pan and place in oven; bake for 45 minutes (or until thermometer reads 170°F), basting occasionally with pan juices. To serve, slice turkey, drizzle with pan juices, and garnish with green onions.

Jerk Chicken

4 whole chicken breasts (8 halves)

Marinade:
1/2 cup white vinegar
  2 Tbsp vegetable oil
1/4 cup soy sauce
  1 tsp allspice
1/2 tsp ground nutmeg
1/2 tsp ground cinnamon
1/2 tsp garlic salt
  1 tsp salt
1/2 cup scallions, chopped
  4 jalapeno chili pepper, stems removed
      (remove seeds for a milder version)

Makes 4 Servings	
Analysis per Serving:	
Carbs	**4.3g**
Calories	232.6
Fat	7.8g
Protein	76.7g

1. Place all of the marinade ingredients into a blender on high speed until completely liquefied.

2. Place chicken in a non-metallic bowl, cover with marinade. Refrigerate over night.

3. Grill chicken about 4 minutes on each side. Serve.

You can also use pork chops, fish or beef. Try using the marinade on beef or pork ribs for a great Caribbean variation!

Mediterranean Chicken

1 tsp oil, for greasing pan
3 lbs roasting chicken
2 large cloves garlic
2 Tbsp green olive oil
1 Tbsp minced fresh tarragon
1 tsp crushed sage
4 Tbsp balsamic vinegar
4 oz pitted Greek olives

Makes 4 Servings	
Analysis per Serving:	
Carbs	**3.9g**
Calories	333.2
Fat	20.5g
Protein	22.5g

Set oven to 375°F. Lightly oil a large roasting pan or deep casserole.

1. Place chicken in roasting pan, breast side up. Peel and halve garlic cloves, rub surface of chicken with cut garlic, then place cloves inside chicken.

2. Mix together olive oil, tarragon, sage, and vinegar. Pour over surface of chicken and inside cavity. Cut and place olives around chicken.

3. Cover pan and place in oven. Roast until juice runs clear when a sharp knife is inserted in thigh of bird (45 minutes to 1 hour). Slice or cut into serving pieces and serve with olives, and cooking liquid.

Oriental Grilled Chicken

2 boneless chicken breasts (or 4 halves)
1/2 cup soy sauce
1 packet Sweet 'n Low®
1/2 cup rice wine
1 Tbsp sesame oil
1 scallion, chopped
1" ginger root, peeled and chopped

Makes 4 Servings	
Analysis per Serving:	
Carbs	**5.0g**
Calories	107.3
Fat	8.8g
Protein	9.8g

1. Cut chicken breasts into halves.

2. Mix remaining ingredients together in a shallow pan large enough to hold breasts in one layer.

3. Place breasts in marinade, turning to coat and rubbing marinade into breasts. Marinate at least one hour and as long as overnight.

4. Grill chicken over hot coals or under broiler.

5. Meanwhile, strain marinade, bring it to a boil, and serve it with chicken.

Roast Duckling with Sherry

2 ducklings (2 to 3 lb each)
1/2 tsp celery salt
1/2 tsp onion salt
1/2 tsp celery seed
1/4 tsp curry powder
  1 tsp herbal salt substitute
1/4 tsp pepper
1/4 cup minced celery
1/2 cup minced onion
1/2 cup sherry

Makes 4 Servings	
Analysis per Serving:	
Carbs	**4.8g**
Calories	607.5
Fat	19.3g
Protein	90.0g

1. Place ducklings in a large Dutch oven, breasts up.

2. In a small bowl mix together celery salt, onion salt, celery seed, curry powder, salt substitute, and pepper. Rub into skin of ducklings. Let marinate 1 hour.

3. Preheat oven to 300°F. Add celery and onion to Dutch oven. Pour in the 1/2 cup sherry.

4. Place Dutch oven over medium-high heat and brown ducklings on both sides (about 20 minutes per side). Cover Dutch oven and bake for 1 hour. Slice and serve.

Turkey Mushroom Melt

1 lb cooked turkey, cubed
2 scallions, diced
4 oz canned mushrooms
1 dash oregano
1 dash sage
1 dash paprika
   salt and pepper to taste
1/3 lb cheddar cheese, grated

Makes 2 Servings	
Analysis per Serving:	
Carbs	**5.3g**
Calories	710.5
Fat	36.6g
Protein	86.8g

Set oven to 350°F

1. Toss together all ingredients except the cheese. Place in baking dish and sprinkle cheese on top.

2. Bake for 15 minutes. Serve.

This can also be heated in a microwave instead.

Fish and Seafood

FISH & SEAFOOD

Baked Haddock
Blackened Fish Fillets
Coquilles St. Jacques
Crab Soufflé
Creamy Dill Salmon - microwave
Grilled Swordfish with Cilantro Butter
Grilled Trout
Lemon Seafood Newburg
Louisiana Grilled Shrimp
Poached Salmon with Ginger
Salmon with Mustard Sauce
Scallops Charlotte
Seafood Au Gratin
Shrimp Scampi
Shrimp St. Jacques
Shrimp Vindaloo
Steamed Mussels
Stir-Fried Shrimp with Ginger and Garlic
Tequila Shrimp Kebabs
Tuna with Wasabi Sauce

Baked Haddock

4 haddock fillets
1/2 cup butter, melted
1 Tbsp lemon juice
2 Tbsp Worcestershire sauce
1/4 tsp ground chili peppers
1 tsp salt
1/4 tsp black pepper
1 garlic clove, minced

Makes 4 Servings	
Analysis per Serving:	
Carbs	**2.1g**
Calories	377.1
Fat	24.1g
Protein	37.0g

Set oven to 375°F

1. Mix salt, pepper and garlic together thoroughly and rub on both sides of fish fillets. Place in a buttered shallow baking dish.

2. Combine butter, lemon juice, and Worcestershire sauce. Pour over fish.

3. Bake fish at 375°F for 30 minutes or until it flakes easily with a fork. Baste with butter mixture 2-3 times during baking.

Blackened Fish Fillets

3 lbs fish fillets, 1/2 to 3/4" thick
3/4 cup butter
1 Tbsp paprika
3/4 tsp cayenne pepper
1 tsp salt
1/2 tsp black pepper
1/2 tsp white pepper
1 tsp onion powder
1 tsp garlic powder
1/2 tsp dried thyme
1/2 tsp dried oregano
1 dash cumin

Makes 6 Servings	
Analysis per Serving:	
Carbs	**1.8g**
Calories	303.9
Fat	23.7g
Protein	21.2g

This is best with a firm fish such as salmon, swordfish, monk fish, etc. but almost any fish can be used.

1. Mix dry ingredients on large plate.

2. Melt butter in heavy skillet. Pour into a 9 x 12 pan.

3. Dip each fillet in melted butter (in the 9 x 12 pan) and then dip in the dry ingredients, patting the fillets by hand.

4. If cooking indoors, TURN ON HOOD VENT and turn heat to high. It is best to cook this on an outdoor grill.

5. Cook fish on each side for 2 to 3 minutes, being careful when turning them over. The fish will look charred -- "blackened" -- and there may be some smoke.

The blackening forms a spicy, crunchy coating, sealing in moisture and flavor.

Coquilles St. Jacques

2 cups chicken stock
1/2 cup white wine
1 bay leaf
2 Tbsp fresh parsley, chopped
1/4 tsp ground thyme
5 whole peppercorns
1/4 tsp fennel seed
2 lbs scallops
8 oz mushrooms, sliced
1 shallot chopped
1/4 cup butter
3 drops lemon extract
1 cup heavy cream
3 egg yolks
1/2 tsp salt

Makes 4 Servings	
Analysis per Serving:	
Carbs	**8.3g**
Calories	426.5
Fat	38.3g
Protein	7.0g

1. Combine chicken stock, wine, bay leaf, parsley, thyme, peppercorns and fennel; bring to a boil and simmer, uncovered for 20-30 minutes.

2. Add scallops and simmer 10 minutes. Remove scallops to a bowl. Strain stock and reduce over high heat to one cup.

3. Sauté sliced mushrooms and shallots in butter until tender. Remove mushrooms and shallots to bowl with scallops. Stir in reduced stock and 3/4 cup cream. Heat just to boiling.

4. Beat egg yolk into remaining cream and add to sauce. Bring up to a boil and remove from heat. Add lemon extract and adjust seasoning.

5. Drain scallop/mushroom mixture and fold in half of the cream sauce.

6. Butter 4 scallop shells or ramekins and place a tablespoon of sauce in each. Divide scallop mixture equally between the 4 dishes and top with remaining sauce. Bake at 375°F for 10 minutes. Serve at once.

Crab Soufflé

8 eggs
1/4 cup heavy cream
8 oz cream cheese
2 scallion, chopped
1 can crab meat
4 oz canned mushrooms
1/4 tsp garlic salt
1/4 tsp paprika
1/8 tsp white pepper
1/4 tsp lemon extract
2 oz cheddar cheese, grated

Makes 6 Servings	
Analysis per Serving:	
Carbs	**8.3g**
Calories	467.8
Fat	36.7g
Protein	27.5g

Preheat oven to 400°F.

1. Beat eggs with cream and seasonings.

2. In a pie pan or 8x8 casserole dish make a layer of 1/2 of the mushrooms, then 1/2 of the scallions, 1/2 of the crab meat and 1/2 of the cream cheese. Repeat.

3. Cover with cheddar cheese and a sprinkle of paprika. Place in center of oven, reduce heat to 350°F and bake for 45 minutes. Let cool for 5 to 10 minutes before cutting and serving.

This is also good served cold.

Creamy Dill Salmon (microwave)

4 salmon fillets
  salt & freshly ground pepper, to taste
2 Tbsp butter
3 tsp fresh dill, finely chopped
1 Tbsp lemon juice
1/4 cup whipping cream
  dill or parsley sprigs, for garnish

Makes 4 Servings	
Analysis per Serving:	
Carbs	**0.8g**
Calories	299.9
Fat	17.1g
Protein	34.3g

1. Place butter in an 8 or 9-inch square glass baking dish. Microwave on 100% power about 45 seconds to melt butter. Stir dill and lemon juice into butter.

2. Arrange fish in a single layer in baking dish, with the thickest portions toward the outside of the dish. Turn to coat both sides with butter. Cover dish with waxed paper.

3. Microwave on 100% power until fish turns from transparent to opaque, 3 to 6 minutes (give dish a quarter turn after 2 minutes if you microwave does not rotate). Check doneness by cutting into center of thickest portion.

4. Place cooked fish on a platter; cover with foil.

5. Stir cream into juices in dish. Microwave on 100% power about 2 minutes. Add salmon juices that have accumulated on dish and microwave 2 to 4 minutes longer, or until sauce thickens and lightly coats a spoon.

6. Spoon sauce over fish. Garnish with dill or parsley.

Grilled Swordfish with Cilantro Butter

4 fresh swordfish fillets
2 Tbsp olive oil

Cilantro Butter:
  1 bunch cilantro
1/2 cup butter
1/4 tsp lemon extract
    salt and freshly ground pepper, to taste

Makes 4 Servings	
Analysis per Serving:	
Carbs	**0.2g**
Calories	482.1
Fat	38.0g
Protein	34.0g

1. Prepare a charcoal fire or gas grill. Swordfish is especially good cooked over mesquite charcoal, although other types of fuel are fine.

2. Lightly coat fillets with olive oil. When fire is ready, place fish on oiled grill and cook until just firm to the touch (about 4 minutes per side for thick fillets, less for thinner fillets; don't overcook). Serve immediately with Cilantro Butter.

3. Cilantro Butter: Wash cilantro thoroughly and remove thick stems. Combine with butter in food processor or blender with metal blade and mix for several seconds until light and fluffy. Blend in lemon juice. Season with salt and pepper.

Grilled Trout

2 trout
2 Tbsp soy sauce
1/2 cup olive oil
2 Tbsp sherry
2 Tbsp lemon juice
1 garlic clove, crushed
1/4 tsp sage

Makes 2 Servings	
Analysis per Serving:	
Carbs	**4.4g**
Calories	656.4
Fat	59.7g
Protein	18.8g

1. Brush trout inside and out with some of the lemon juice to preserve freshness.

2. Mix well all ingredients (except trout).

3. Place trout in a small container, pour marinade over trout and refrigerate for 1 hour.

4. Place trout on grill and cook until done (~15 minutes). Baste frequently with marinade. Serve.

Lemon Seafood Newburg

1/2 lb shrimp, shells removed
1 lb crab legs (King or Snow)
1/2 lb scallops
3 Tbsp butter
1 cup heavy cream
3 egg yolks
1 garlic clove, minced fine
1 Tbsp sherry
1/2 tsp lemon extract
1/2 tsp paprika
1 Tbsp chives, minced

Makes 4 Servings	
Analysis per Serving:	
Carbs	**4.5g**
Calories	538.3
Fat	36.5g
Protein	45.3g

1. Remove crab meat from legs and set aside.

2. Melt butter and sauté garlic. Add sherry and lemon juice.

3. Beat egg yolks, add cream and beat again.

4. Over medium heat, slowly pour egg mixture into butter mixture, stirring constantly until thicken.

5. Add scallops and reduce heat to lowest setting. Let cook for 5 minutes. Add shrimp and cook another 5 minutes.

6. Heat 4 large ramekin in microwave with a little water. Remove ramekin, pour off water, divide the crab between the two, pour in the Newburg sauce. Garnish with chives. Serve immediately.

As an alternative, prepare as above except do not use the ramekins. Gently stir the crab meat into the Newburg sauce and then pour across steamed asparagus (in a nice neat line, 90 degrees to the asparagus spears). This makes an elegant presentation.

Louisiana Grilled Shrimp

1 lb large shrimp
1/2 cup olive oil
1/2 tsp lemon extract
1 tsp Cajun seasoning
1 Tbsp Worcestershire sauce
1 large bell pepper, cut into 2" pieces
1/4 cup butter, melted
1 dash Tabasco sauce

Makes 3 Servings	
Analysis per Serving:	
Carbs	**5.1g**
Calories	629.4
Fat	53.9g
Protein	31.4g

1. Place un-peeled shrimp in 2 quart casserole.

2. Mix together olive oil, lemon extract, Cajun seasoning, and Worcestershire sauce. Drizzle over shrimp and marinate for at least 4 hours.

3. Remove from marinade and skewer with chunks of bell pepper. Mix butter and Tabasco sauce and brush over shrimp. Grill over hot coals until browned.

Finger lickin' good!

Poached Salmon with Ginger

1 lb salmon fillet
1 Tbsp ginger root, grated
3 lemon slices
3 Tbsp dry white wine
1 Tbsp lemon juice

Makes 2 Servings	
Analysis per Serving:	
Carbs	**5.8g**
Calories	305.5
Fat	8.0g
Protein	45.9g

Set oven to 375°F

1. Place salmon fillet on 2 layers of aluminum foil, large enough to make a tent over the fish.

2. Rub ginger into salmon, cover with slices of lemon. Sprinkle wine and lemon juice over the fish. Fold foil so that it makes a tent with the ends sealed too.

3. Place on baking sheet and bake at 375°F for 20 minutes (or longer if fillet is thicker than 1 inch). Carefully unfold the top of the foil. Transfer fish to serving platter. Pour cooking juices over fish and serve.

Salmon with Mustard Sauce

4 large salmon steaks
1/4 cup dry white wine
1 minced shallot
2 Tbsp minced fresh dill
1/4 cup sour cream
1/4 cup Dijon mustard
1 packet Sweet 'n Low®
1/2 tsp lemon extract

Makes 4 Servings	
Analysis per Serving:	
Carbs	**2.8g**
Calories	254.0
Fat	9.6g
Protein	35.3g

Set oven to 400°F.

1. Place salmon steaks in a large, deep baking pan and cover with wine. Sprinkle with shallots. Bake for 12 to 15 minutes, basting often with wine.

2. While salmon is baking, in a small bowl mix together dill, sour cream, mustard, sweetener, and lemon extract until smooth. Serve over salmon at room temperature.

Scallops Charlotte

2 lbs scallops
2 Tbsp butter
2 Tbsp shallots, finely chopped
1/2 lb small mushrooms, sliced
3/4 cup whipping cream
4 Tbsp Marsala wine
salt and white pepper to taste,
finely chopped chives or parsley, for garnish

Makes 6 Servings	
Analysis per Serving:	
Carbs	**4.2g**
Calories	167.6
Fat	15.0g
Protein	2.2g

1. If you are using large sea scallops, you may want to cut them in half horizontally. If you have tiny bay scallops, they can be left whole.

2. In a large skillet over medium heat, melt 1 Tbsp of the butter. Add shallots and mushrooms; sauté over medium-high heat for 2 minutes. Remove to a bowl and set aside.

3. Melt remaining butter in skillet. Add scallops. Sauté 2 to 3 minutes, until scallops are opaque. Using a slotted spoon, remove scallops from skillet and add them to mushroom mixture; set aside.

4. Add cream and wine to liquid in skillet. Add any juices that have accumulated in bowl of scallops.

5. Cook, stirring constantly, over medium heat until sauce reduces to 2/3 to 3/4 cup and thickens enough to lightly coat a spoon.

6. Add mushroom and scallop mixture; cook to heat through. Season to taste with salt and pepper. Serve garnished with chives.

Seafood Au Gratin

1/2 lb mushrooms, sliced
1 whole shallot, chopped
6 Tbsp butter
3/4 cup heavy cream
1 Tbsp brandy
salt
black pepper
paprika
1/2 lb crab meat, cooked
1/2 cup lobster meat, cooked
1/2 lb large shrimp, cooked & peeled
1/4 cup Parmesan cheese

Makes 4 Servings	
Analysis per Serving:	
Carbs	5.8g
Calories	495.9
Fat	37.2g
Protein	33.0g

Set oven to 450°F

1. In a medium skillet, sauté mushrooms and shallots in butter for five minutes.

2. Beat egg yolk into cream and add to skillet slowly, stirring constantly. Remove from heat when thickened and stir in brandy. Season with salt, pepper, and paprika., to taste

3. Place crab meat, lobster meat, and shrimp in a shallow, buttered casserole dish. Cover with the mushroom-cream sauce and sprinkle with cheese. Bake at 450°F for 10 minutes, then brown under broiler (2-3 minutes).

Shrimp Scampi

2 lbs large shrimp, peeled
1 egg, beaten
salt
pepper
cayenne
1/2 cup olive oil
4 cloves garlic, minced
2 shallots, chopped
1/2 cup parsley, minced
1/2 tsp oregano
2 Tbsp wine
1 Tbsp brandy

Makes 4 Servings	
Analysis per Serving:	
Carbs	**4.9g**
Calories	304.0
Fat	28.5g
Protein	4.0g

1. Season egg with salt, pepper, and cayenne. Dredge shrimp in egg. Sauté shrimp in olive oil for 5 minutes over high heat, shaking briskly. Remove shrimp with a slotted spoon to a shallow casserole dish.

2. Add garlic, shallots, parsley, and oregano to olive oil, sauté over medium heat for 3 minutes, shaking the pan briskly. Remove herbs with a slotted spoon to casserole.

3. Add wine and brandy to skillet and ignite. When flames die down, pour sauce over shrimp. Broil for 2 minutes.

Shrimp St. Jacques

2 lbs shrimp, peeled and de-veined
1/4 cup butter
1/2 lb mushrooms, sliced
1.5 cups sour cream
1 Tbsp chives, chopped
1/2 Tbsp fresh parsley, chopped
1/2 tsp paprika
   salt
   black pepper
1/4 cup Parmesan cheese, grated

Makes 4 Servings	
Analysis per Serving:	
Carbs	**6.7g**
Calories	328.0
Fat	31.3g
Protein	7.2g

1. Sauté shrimp in butter for 3 minutes, add the mushrooms and sauté until tender. Blend in sour cream, parsley, and chives. Season with salt, pepper, and paprika to taste. Cook 5 minutes, stirring continuously.

2. Spoon into 4 scallop shells, sprinkle tops with Parmesan cheese and broil for 3-5 minutes, until tops are golden.

Shrimp Vindaloo

2 lbs large shrimp, cooked & shelled
2 Tbsp ghee (or butter)
1 cup onion, chopped
1 Tbsp ginger, grated
2 Tbsp ground coriander
2 tsp turmeric
3 Tbsp wine vinegar
1 tsp salt
1 can coconut milk, unsweetened
1 packet Sweet 'n Low®
1/4 tsp lemon extract

Makes 6 Servings	
Analysis per Serving:	
Carbs	**4.1g**
Calories	78.7
Fat	6.6g
Protein	2.0g

1. Heat ghee in large skillet and sauté onions for 2 minutes.

2. Add ginger, coriander and turmeric. Reduce the heat to medium and cook for 2 minutes.

3. Add vinegar and salt, stir. Add shrimp stir until well coated. Add coconut milk, sweetener and lemon extract. Simmer for 10 minutes.

Steamed Mussels

24 mussels, scrubbed well
1 Tbsp chopped onion
1 clove garlic, chopped
1 Tbsp chopped celery
1/4 tsp thyme
10 whole peppercorns
1/2 tsp fresh parsley chopped
1 cup water
1/2 cup Chablis
2 Tbsp heavy cream
1 egg yolk

Makes 6 Servings	
Analysis per Serving:	
Carbs	**6.0g**
Calories	511.8
Fat	46.2g
Protein	14.7g

1. Place mussels in basket of steamer.

2. Combine onion, garlic, celery, thyme, peppercorns, and parsley with water and Chablis in bottom of steamer. Steam over high heat until shells open. Remove mussels to warm plate, discarding any that have not opened.

3. Strain broth and boil over high heat until reduced to 1 cup. Beat egg yolk into cream. Add to broth slowly and cook, stirring, until sauce thickens. Serve.

Notes:
1. I prefer New Zealand green lip mussels.
2. This is nice served over spaghetti squash for a little meal.

Stir-Fried Shrimp with Ginger & Garlic

1/4 cup dry white wine
2 Tbsp soy sauce
1 tsp vinegar
1 pinch Sweet 'n Low®
1 lb shrimp, peeled and de-veined
1 Tbsp ginger, minced
1 Tbsp garlic, minced
2 Tbsp green onion, minced
3 Tbsp peanut oil

Makes 4 Servings	
Analysis per Serving:	
Carbs	**4.3g**
Calories	235.4
Fat	12.2g
Protein	23.9g

1. Combine wine, soy sauce, vinegar, and sweetener in a bowl large enough to marinate the shrimp. Toss shrimp in marinade and set aside for 20 minutes or so.

2. Combine ginger, garlic, and green onion in another bowl and set aside.

3. Have all the ingredients and tools at hand and the rest of the dinner ready to serve.

4. Remove shrimp from marinade and drain well, reserving marinade.

5. Heat a wok or large skillet over medium-high heat. When pan is hot, add oil in a thin stream around pan and let it run into center. Add ginger, garlic, green onion mixture to pan, adjust heat so mixture sizzles but does not burn, and stir-fry until very fragrant, about 30 seconds. Add drained shrimp and stir-fry until they begin to stiffen, about 30 seconds. Pour in marinade; stir and cook until liquid is nearly all evaporated. Transfer shrimp to a serving dish and serve immediately.

Tequila Shrimp Kebabs

2 lb Shrimp
1 green bell pepper
1 red bell pepper
8 mushroom caps
1/4 yellow onion
8 slices bacon
2 Tbsp tequila
2 Tbsp oil
1 Tbsp lime juice
Tabasco sauce, to taste

Makes 4 Servings	
Analysis per Serving:	
Carbs	**8.7g**
Calories	420.8
Fat	17.3g
Protein	51.8g

1. Remove shells from shrimp. De-vein if needed.

2. Mix tequila, lime juice, oil and Tabasco.

3. Cut peppers and onions in to 1 1/2 inch squares. Marinate shrimp, mushrooms, peppers and onions for at 1 hour in refrigerator.

4. Wrap a piece of bacon around each shrimp. Skewer, alternating items.

5. Grill for 6 minutes (3 minutes per side). Baste with marinade as needed.

Note: if mushrooms break while being skewered, wrap them in bacon too.

Tuna with Wasabi

2 Tuna steak
1 tsp wasabi
1 tsp water
1 Tbsp white wine
2 tsp soy sauce
1 Tbsp heavy cream

Makes 2 Servings	
Analysis per Serving:	
Carbs	**0.8g**
Calories	278.8
Fat	11.1g
Protein	40.2g

1. Grill tuna to your liking. Usually 4 minutes per side for 1 inch thick steaks.

2. Mix wasabi and water to form a paste. Add all other ingredients, mix well.

3. Pour sauce over grilled tuna steaks and serve.

Soups and Stews

SOUPS & STEWS

Avocado Soup
Beef Stew
Broccoli Cheddar Cheese Soup
Chilled Cucumber Soup
Crab Chowder
Cream of Artichoke & Mushroom Soup
Cream of Cauliflower Soup
Cream of Mushroom Soup
Creamy Chicken Soup
Ginger Crab Soup
Leek Soup
Lobster Stew
Salmon Chowder
Seafood Bouillabaisse
Shrimp Bisque
Spinach Soup
Spinach Cream Soup
Thai Ginger Chicken Soup
Tomato Cheddar Soup
Turkey Mushroom Soup

Avocado Soup

2 avocados
2 drops lemon extract
2 cups chicken broth
1 Tbsp dry sherry
1 cup heavy cream
  salt, to taste
  cayenne pepper, to taste

Makes 6 Servings	
Analysis per Serving:	
Carbs	**6.7g**
Calories	273.4
Fat	25.8g
Protein	5.8g

Peel and pit avocados. Puree in a blender with lemon extract. Blend in chicken broth and sherry. Pour into a bowl and whisk in cream. Season to taste with salt and cayenne. Chill.

Beef Stew

2 lbs beef stew meat
3 Tbsp olive oil
1 packet Sweet 'n Low®, optional
1 celery stalk, diced
1 Tbsp parsley sprigs, chopped
1 garlic clove minced
1 whole bay leaf
4 cups beef stock
3 scallions, chopped

Makes 6 Servings	
Analysis per Serving:	
Carbs	**2.1g**
Calories	208.3
Fat	13.4g
Protein	16.7g

1. In a large skillet, brown meat in hot olive oil. Put meat in a slow cooker.

2. Pour stock into a sauce pan and bring to a boil. Par boil the celery, garlic, and scallions for 2 minutes.

3. Pour stock & vegetables into slow cooker. Add herbs, cover and cook on low heat (do not boil) for 4 - 8 hours. Remove bay leaf before serving.

Broccoli Cheddar Cheese Soup

10 oz (1 can) beef broth
2 cup heavy cream
1/4 cup white wine
1 tsp Worcestershire sauce
1/4 tsp garlic powder, to taste
Salt, if needed, to taste
Black pepper, to taste
1 cup celery, finely minced
2 cups coarsely chopped broccoli florets
1 cup grated cheddar cheese
1 Tbsp minced parsley or dill, as garnish (optional)

Makes 6 Servings	
Analysis per Serving:	
Carbs	**5.2g**
Calories	396.7
Fat	36.6g
Protein	12.0g

1. Add broth, celery, cream, wine, Worcestershire sauce, garlic, salt & pepper to a soup kettle. Bring to a boil.

2. Add broccoli (make sure that broccoli is cut into bite sized pieces), then lower heat and simmer for 20 minutes or until broccoli is beginning to become tender.

3. When broccoli is just about done to proper tenderness, slowly add grated cheddar cheese, stirring constantly until each bit is completely blended into soup.

4. Before serving, garnish with a sprinkle of parsley or fresh dill.

Chilled Cucumber Soup

1 lg cucumber
1 cup heavy cream
1/2 cup plain yogurt
2 Tbsp tarragon vinegar
2 garlic clove, finely minced
3 fresh basil leaves, chopped
1/4 tsp dried tarragon
salt and pepper to taste

Makes 4 Servings	
Analysis per Serving:	
Carbs	8.2g
Calories	246.9
Fat	23.2g
Protein	3.4g

1. Scrub cucumber to remove any wax, but do not peel.

2. Coarsely grate cucumber and place in a large bowl. Capture as much liquid as possible.

3. Add remaining ingredients and hand mix.

4. Chill for at least 1 hour prior to serving. Garnish with a sprig of parsley, a sprinkle of fresh chopped chives or a dash of paprika.

Crab Chowder

10 oz frozen or fresh cauliflower
1 cup water
7 oz canned crab meat
2 Tbsp scallions, chopped
2 Tbsp pimiento
3 cups heavy cream
3 oz cream cheese
1/2 tsp salt
1/2 tsp white pepper
1/2 tsp paprika

Makes 6 Servings	
Analysis per Serving:	
Carbs	**6.5g**
Calories	506.5
Fat	49.5g
Protein	11.4g

1. In a large sauce pan, heat water until boiling. Add cauliflower and return to boil. Cook 2 minutes. Cut up any large pieces. Add cream, scallions and pimento. Heat and stir just until boiling (do not boil).

2. Add crab, cream cheese, salt, pepper and paprika. Heat until cream cheese melts and chowder is hot (do not boil). Serve.

Cream of Artichoke & Mushroom Soup

1 can artichoke hearts
10 oz fresh mushrooms
2 Tbsp butter
1 garlic clove, minced
1 Tbsp celery, finely minced
12 oz chicken stock
2 cups heavy cream
4 egg yolk
1 Tbsp, sherry
   salt and pepper, to taste

Makes 6 Servings	
Analysis per Serving:	
Carbs	**6.8g**
Calories	374.5
Fat	36.8g
Protein	5.2g

1. Melt butter and sauté mushrooms, garlic and celery until just tender, about 3 minutes.

2. Slice each artichoke heart into 4ths or 6ths. Reserve liquid.

3. Combine mushrooms, artichokes and liquid with stock and sherry in a soup kettle. Season with salt and pepper to taste. Bring to a boil then reduce heat and simmer 5 minutes.

4. Beat egg yolks, add cream and beat again. Pour about 1/2 cup of soup broth into cream, mix well. Then blend egg mixture into the rest of the soup, pouring in a slow, steady stream, and stirring constantly.

5. Simmer for 30 minutes, but do not allow to boil. Serve.

This is one of my favorites soups and is great year-around! It's best the second day.

Cream of Cauliflower Soup

1 head cauliflower
1/4 cup butter
2 Tbsp onion, chopped
3 stalks celery, minced
4 cups chicken stock
2 cups heavy cream
1/8 tsp nutmeg
1/8 tsp paprika
  salt to taste
3 oz cheddar cheese, grated

Makes 6 Servings	
Analysis per Serving:	
Carbs	**9.4g**
Calories	609.8
Fat	56.0g
Protein	17.5g

1. Steam whole cauliflower (all leaves removed and stem trimmed slightly). Cool until it can be handled safely.

2. Break off florets. Put stems in food processor or blender with enough of the steaming water to blend into a paste.

3. Sauté onions and celery in butter until tender. Add chicken stock, nutmeg, paprika and cauliflower paste, bring to a boil.

4. Reduce heat and add cream and cauliflower florets, heat but do not boil for about 2 minutes.

5. Serve with cheese as a garnish.

Cream of Mushroom Soup

16 oz fresh mushrooms
2 Tbsp butter
1 garlic clove, minced
2 cups chicken stock
2 cups heavy cream
4 egg yolk
1 Tbsp sherry, to taste
   salt and pepper, to taste

Makes 6 Servings	
Analysis per Serving:	
Carbs	**6.5g**
Calories	376.4
Fat	37.0g
Protein	5.4g

1. Clean mushrooms, separating caps and stems. Slice half of the caps crosswise into 1/8" slices. Chop stems and remaining caps.

2. Melt butter and sauté mushrooms, garlic and celery until just tender, about 3 minutes.

3. Combine mushrooms with stock and sherry in a medium saucepan. Season with salt and pepper to taste. Bring to a boil then reduce heat and simmer 5 minutes.

4. Beat egg yolks, add cream and mix well. Pour about 1/2 cup of soup broth into cream, mix well. Then blend egg mixture into the rest of the soup, pouring in a slow, steady stream, and stirring constantly.

5. Simmer for 30 minutes, but do not allow to boil.

Garnish with chopped scallions or chives for very little extra carbs.

Creamy Chicken Soup

1 chicken, roasted
1 cup celery, chopped
1 garlic clove, crushed
4 oz mushroom, chopped
2 scallions, chopped
1 Tbsp butter
2 cups heavy cream
3 egg yolks
1 Tbsp white wine
1/4 tsp pepper
1/4 tsp oregano

Makes 6 Servings	
Analysis per Serving:	
Carbs	**4.7g**
Calories	828.4
Fat	68.0g
Protein	45.8g

1. De-bone roasted chicken and cut meat into small bite size pieces.

2. Chicken Stock: Place chicken bones & skin in 3 cups of water, add 1 tsp of salt. Boil until reduced to approximately 2 cups. This will take about 20 to 30 minutes. Make stock while preparing other ingredients.

3. In a soup kettle, sauté in butter the celery, garlic, pepper and oregano for 2 minutes. Add mushrooms and sauté for 1 more minute. Add chicken and stock. Bring to a boil. Reduce heat to medium.

4. Beat egg yolks with cream. Add 1/2 cup of stock to cream mix well. Slowly pour cream into soup, stirring constantly until slightly thickened. Add wine & scallions. Simmer for 15 minutes. Serve.

Ginger Crab Soup

3 cups homemade chicken stock
2 thin slices fresh ginger root, un-peeled
6 oz fresh or frozen crab meat, thawed
1 green onion, chopped
1 Tbsp dry sherry
1 tsp white vinegar
   salt and cayenne pepper, to taste

Makes 4 Servings	
Analysis per Serving:	
Carbs	**3.1g**
Calories	207.0
Fat	2.4g
Protein	37.5g

1. In a medium saucepan, bring chicken stock and ginger to a simmer.

2. Remove pan from heat and remove ginger slices.

3. Stir in crab meat and green onions. Season to taste with sherry, vinegar, salt, and cayenne.

Leek Soup

3 leeks
4 cups chicken stock
   salt
   black pepper
   ground nutmeg
1 cup heavy cream
1 egg yolk

Makes 6 Servings	
Analysis per Serving:	
Carbs	**6.6g**
Calories	199.1
Fat	15.8g
Protein	2.8g

1. Clean and trim leeks, using mostly only the white part (a little of the green is good for color but that's where the carbs are). Slice thinly.

2. Bring chicken stock to a boil. Reduce heat, add leeks and simmer for about five minutes, until just tender. Season with salt, pepper, and nutmeg to taste.

3. Beat egg yolk with cream and pour in a thin stream into simmering stock. Stir until blended. Serve at once.

Lobster Stew

2 whole Maine lobsters, cooked
1 medium onion
2 cups heavy cream
1/2 cup water
1 celery stalk
1 bay leaf
1 Tbsp whole cloves
2 Tbsp sherry
   salt, to taste
   black pepper, to taste
   nutmeg, to taste
1 egg yolk, beaten
1/4 tsp lemon extract
2 Tbsp butter

Makes 4 Servings	
Analysis per Serving:	
Carbs	**6.3g**
Calories	570.2
Fat	52.0g
Protein	17.5g

1. Remove meat from lobster and reserve shell.

2. Stud onion all over with whole cloves. Break up lobster shells and place in soup kettle with water, onion, celery, and bay leaf. Simmer 45 minutes.

3. Meanwhile make lemon butter. Let butter come to room temperature. Mix lemon extract into butter. Refrigerate until ready to serve.

4. Strain broth through sieve into a clean soup kettle. Add lobster meat and sherry. Season to taste with salt, pepper, cayenne, and nutmeg. Simmer over very low heat until lobster is heated through.

5. Beat cream and 1/2 cup of the soup broth into beaten egg yolk. Pour egg mixture gradually into remaining soup mixture and heat 1-2 minutes longer.

6. Pour into soup bowls and top each with 1/2 Tbsp lemon butter.

Salmon Chowder

3 Tbsp butter
2 shallots, slivered
1 tsp dried tarragon
1/2 tsp salt
1/8 tsp white pepper
2 cups chicken stock
2 lbs salmon steaks, 3/4 to 1 inch thick
1/8 tsp lemon extract
1 bay leaf
1/2 cup dry white wine
1/4 lb bacon slices, cut in 1/2-inch pieces
1/4 small cabbage, cored and shredded
1 cup whipping cream

Makes 6 Servings	
Analysis per Serving:	
Carbs	**6.3g**
Calories	426.8
Fat	33.7g
Protein	19.0g

1. In a large pot or Dutch oven over medium heat, melt butter; add shallots and cook, stirring, until soft but not browned. Mix in tarragon. Add broth, bay leaf and lemon extract and bring to a boil over medium-high heat. Cover, reduce heat to medium.

2. Add salmon steaks in a single layer; pour in wine. Cover and cook over low heat until salmon flakes when tested with a fork (10 to 12 minutes).

3. Meanwhile, in a medium skillet, cook bacon in its own drippings until lightly browned. Remove from heat, drain on paper towel. Break each into bits.

4. Remove and discard bay leaf. Remove salmon steaks; discard salmon bones and skin and divide salmon into chunks and set aside.

5. Add cabbage and cream to soup. Stir occasionally over medium heat until cabbage is wilted and bright green (3 to 5 minutes). Gently mix in salmon. Taste, and add salt if needed.

6. Serve chowder hot, spooning several pieces of bacon into each bowl.

Seafood Bouillabaisse

2 Tbsp butter
2 Tbsp olive oil
1/2 cup onion, chopped
1/2 cup celery, chopped
1 clove garlic, minced
4 cups fish stock or clam juice
10 oz canned tomatoes
1/4 cup white wine
1 Tbsp lemon juice
2 Tbsp parsley
1 whole bay leaf
1/2 tsp salt
1/4 tsp cayenne pepper
2 lbs fish fillets, cut in 1" chunks
1 lb shrimp, peeled and de-veined
1 cup crab meat, fresh or canned

Makes 8 Servings	
Analysis per Serving:	
Carbs	**6.3g**
Calories	221.9
Fat	8.1g
Protein	28.7g

1. Melt butter with olive oil in a large pot. Sauté onion, celery, and garlic until vegetables are tender.

2. Stir fish stock or clam juice, stock, tomatoes, wine, lemon juice, herbs, and seasonings. Simmer on low heat for 20 minutes.

3. Add fish and cook for 10 minutes. Add shrimp and crab meat; cook 5 more minutes. Serve hot.

Shrimp Bisque

1 lb shrimp, cooked & shelled
1 shallot, minced
1 Tbsp butter
1 Tbsp celery, finely minced
1 cup chicken stock
2 cups heavy cream
4 egg yolks
1/2 tsp paprika
1 Tbsp sherry
1 Tbsp lemon juice
1 Tbsp chives, chopped
   salt and pepper to taste

Makes 4 Servings	
Analysis per Serving:	
Carbs	**6.9g**
Calories	632.6
Fat	54.0g
Protein	28.8g

1. If using medium to large shrimp then cut them into smaller pieces. If using canned or cocktail shrimp you can leave them whole.

2. In soup pan, sauté in butter the celery and shallots for 2 minutes. Add chicken stock, sherry and lemon juice. Bring to a boil. Reduce heat to medium.

3. Beat egg yolks with cream and paprika. Add 1/2 cup of stock to cream and mix well. Slowly pour cream into soup pan stirring constantly until thickened. Reduce heat to a simmer.

4. Remove about 1/2 cup of the broth and place in blender with about 1/8 of the shrimp. Blend until smooth.

5. Return it to soup pan and stir. Add remainder of shrimp and the chives. Add salt & pepper, to taste. Heat through (approx. 5 minutes) and serve.

Spinach Soup

4 cups homemade chicken stock
1 bunch fresh spinach, rinsed & stemmed
1/3 cup heavy cream
2 tsp fresh dill, finely chopped
salt and black pepper, to taste

Makes 4 Servings	
Analysis per Serving:	
Carbs	**2.0g**
Calories	93.5
Fat	7.6g
Protein	1.7g

1. In a medium saucepan, bring stock to a boil.

2. Place spinach in food processor fitted with the steel blade, or in a blender. Add about 2 cups stock to spinach. Process ~ 60 seconds.

3. Return spinach mixture to saucepan. Stir in remaining stock and the cream. Cook until soup is heated through. Season to taste with dill, salt, and pepper.

Spinach Cream Soup

10 oz frozen spinach, chopped
2 cups heavy cream
2 cups chicken stock
1 garlic clove, crushed
1 tbsp butter
1/8 tsp nutmeg
1/2 pkg Sweet 'n Low® sweetener, optional
salt and pepper, to taste

Makes 4 Servings	
Analysis per Serving:	
Carbs	**7.1g**
Calories	465.9
Fat	47.2g
Protein	5.0g

1. Defrost spinach (I zap it in the microwave).

2. In a large sauce pan, cook the garlic in the butter for one minute.

3. Place all ingredients (including the garlic) in a blender and blend to desired consistency. Return to sauce pan and heat just to the boiling point (do not boil). Serve immediately.

This soup is so quick and easy - only minutes to prepare! Even if you don't care much for spinach, try this recipe; the nutmeg gives it a great taste!

Thai Ginger Chicken Soup

2 garlic clove, crushed
1 Tbsp ginger root, grated
2 tsp, lemon grass, ground
1 Tbsp coriander, ground
1/8 tsp cayenne pepper
1 Tbsp ghee or butter
1 chicken, cooked , de-boned
14 oz coconut milk, canned (unsweetened)
2 tsp Nellie & Joe's Key Lime Juice
2 cups chicken stock
1 packet Sweet 'n Low®
1/4 cup cilantro, fresh & chopped

Makes 4 Servings	
Analysis per Serving:	
Carbs	**4.4g**
Calories	249.3
Fat	18.9g
Protein	13.3g

1. De-bone roasted chicken and cut meat into small bite sized pieces.

2. Chicken Stock: Place chicken bones & skin in 3 cups of water, add 2 tsp of salt. Boil until reduced to approximately 2 cups. This will take about 20 to 30 minutes. Make stock while preparing other ingredients. Alternatively, you can use 2 cups of canned chicken stock.

3. In soup pan, melt ghee on medium heat. Add & sauté garlic, lemon grass, coriander and cayenne for one minute. Add ginger and sauté 1 minute (careful not to burn). Add lime juice & sauté 1 minute. (This step is important to do in the order listed).

4. Add coconut milk, and chicken and bring to a slow boil. Add chicken stock, cilantro and Sweet-n-Low, simmer for at least 10 minutes. Serve.

Notes:
1. This is my favorite soup!
2. If you don't have Nellie & Joe's Key Lime Juice, substitute twice the amount of fresh lime juice.
3. This soup can sit on low heat as long as needed. Second & third day, it's just as good!

Tomato Cheddar Soup

3 whole fresh tomatoes
1 stalk celery, diced
3 cups chicken stock
2 scallions, minced
1 cup heavy cream
1 tsp ground basil
1/4 tsp onion salt
1/4 tsp black pepper
8 oz cheddar cheese, shredded

Makes 6 Servings	
Analysis per Serving:	
Carbs	**7.2g**
Calories	773.2
Fat	65.1g
Protein	39.6g

1. Combine tomatoes, and celery in food processor and blend until coarsely chopped.

2. Pour into large saucepan, add chicken stock and scallions, and bring to a boil over medium heat. Simmer, uncovered, for 20 minutes.

3. Add cream. Season with basil, salt, and pepper. Cook over very low heat for five minutes. Add cheese and cook, stirring constantly, until cheese melts. Serve at once.

Turkey Mushroom Soup

1 lb cooked turkey
1 cup mushrooms, chopped
2 scallions, chopped
1/2 cup red bell pepper, chopped
4 cups chicken stock
1 Tbsp white wine
1 Tbsp butter
1 tsp dried basil
   dash oregano
   dash sage
   salt & pepper, to taste

Makes 4 Servings	
Analysis per Serving:	
Carbs	**3.6g**
Calories	254.4
Fat	8.8g
Protein	34.9g

In a large soup pan, melt butter and sauté mushroom, green onions and bell pepper until tender but not brown. Add remaining ingredients. Bring to a boil and then immediately reduce heat to lowest setting for just a few minutes. Serve.

Notes:
1. This soup can sit on low heat for an hour if necessary.
2. Freezes beautifully.

Sauces
and Salad
Dressings

SAUCES & SALAD DRESSINGS

Avocado Cream Sauce
Barbecue Sauce
Bearnaise Sauce - Eggless
Blue Cheese Dressing
Brown Gravy
Cheese Sauce
Cheese Sauce Mexicana
Cowboy Sauce
Creamy Dill Sauce
Cucumber Sauce
Green Chili Sauce
Green Goddess Dressing
Hollandaise Sauce
Hollandaise Sauce, Quick & Easy
Lemon Mayonnaise Sauce/Dressing
Newburg Sauce
Oriental Dressing
Pesto Sauce
Salsa de Cilantro
Spicy Peanut Sauce
Tartar Sauce
Thousand Island Dressing

Avocado Cream Sauce

2 avocados, peeled and seed removed
1 clove garlic, quartered
1 Tbsp fresh chives, chopped
1 Tbsp fresh cilantro, chopped
1/2 Tbsp fresh tarragon, chopped
1/8 tsp lemon extract
2 Tbsp butter
1/4 cup heavy cream

Makes 4 Servings	
Analysis per Serving:	
Carbs	**8.1g**
Calories	265.0
Fat	26.6g
Protein	2.4g

1. In food processor or blender, puree avocado with garlic, lemon extract, and herbs.

2. Melt butter in a saucepan over low heat. Stir in avocado puree and cook over low heat, stirring occasionally, until heated through. Add cream and continue to heat, but do not allow to boil.

3. Salt to taste and serve.

Makes about 1/2 cup.

Barbecue Sauce

2 Tbsp tomato paste
3 Tbsp cooking oil
1 Tbsp water
2 tsp red wine vinegar
2 tsp worcestershire sauce
2 tsp liquid Barbecue Smoke®
2 tsp Kitchen Bouquet
1 tsp Nellie & Joe's Key Lime Juice
1/2 tsp fresh ground black pepper
1 dash garlic powder
   Tabasco sauce, to taste
   salt, to taste

Makes 4 Servings	
Analysis per Serving:	
Carbs	**4.1g**
Calories	109.4
Fat	10.3g
Protein	0.5g

Mix together all ingredients. Refrigerate for at least one hour so that all the flavors can meld.

Notes:
1. Makes about 1/2 cup. One serving is 2 tablespoons.
2. If you prefer your barbecue sauce sweet rather than tangy, then eliminate the lime juice and add 1/2 packet of artificial sweetener.
3. There are so few commercial barbecue sauces that are low in carbs, because they are usually loaded with sugars or molasses. Check your labels! The lowest I've seen is "Stubb's Bar-B-Q Sauce" at 6g carbs for a 2 tablespoon serving.
4. I love barbecued ribs, steaks, burgers, chicken and even fish! I usually make a double, tripe or even quadruple batch and keep it in the refrigerator for up to 1 week.

Bearnaise Sauce - Eggless

2 oz thinly sliced shallots
1 Tbsp dry white wine
1 Tbsp white wine vinegar
1 tsp dried tarragon
1 dash salt & pepper
1/2 cup sour cream

Makes 4 Servings	
Analysis per Serving:	
Carbs	**3.9g**
Calories	75.2
Fat	6.1g
Protein	1.3g

1. Combine all ingredients except sour cream in a small, heavy saucepan; bring to a boil, and cook 1 minute. Strain mixture, reserving liquid; discard solids.

2. Return liquid to saucepan; stir in sour cream. Place over low heat, and cook 1 minute or until warm, stirring frequently.

Notes:
1. Makes about 3/4 cup. Serving size is 3 Tbsp.
2. This eggless version can be made a day in advance & reheated later.

Blue Cheese Dressing

1/4 cup blue cheese, crumbled
1 Tbsp sherry vinegar
1/4 cup mayonnaise
1/2 cup heavy cream
1/8 tsp fresh ground black pepper

Makes 4 Servings	
Analysis per Serving:	
Carbs	**1.3g**
Calories	231.6
Fat	25.1g
Protein	2.6g

1. Crumble blue cheese.

2. In a blender, blend vinegar and mayonnaise. With blender running, slowly add cream. Season with pepper.

3. Fold in blue cheese. Refrigerate 30 minutes.

Makes about 1 cup. One serving is 4 tablespoons.

Brown Gravy

2 Tbsp butter
1 Tbsp flour (yes, you read that right)
2 cups pan drippings or reduced stock
1/2 tsp Kitchen Bouquet

Makes 4 Servings	
Analysis per Serving:	
Carbs	**2.3g**
Calories	70.0
Fat	5.8g
Protein	0.7g

1. To make a roux: melt butter in sauce pan (until it bubbles) and then remove from heat.

2. Add flour and stir well (until no lumps). Add about 1/2 cup of pan drippings or reduced stock. Mix well until there are no lumps.

3. Return to high heat and add remaining pan drippings or stock. Stir well. Add Kitchen Bouquet, stir and bring to a boil until thickened. Serve over meat.

Makes 2 cups. One serving is 1/2 cup. That's a lot of gravy.

Notes:
1. This gravy approach is great with beef and pork roasts. I use it a lot.
2. If you want your gravy thicker, double the butter & flour, but double the carbs as well.
3. For poultry, use less Kitchen Bouquet or simply eliminate it.
4. There are two ways to get reduced stock. One is to add the stock to the beef, pork or poultry while it is baking and the stock will reduce by itself while it cooks (I prefer this method). The other way is to pour twice the amount in a sauce pan and boil it to ½ the volume.
5. Dr. Atkins suggests making gravies using egg yolk. This is fine sometimes, but I prefer the old fashion way using a roux (as above). They say that using flour on this diet can trigger cravings for complex carbohydrates, but my gravies don't seem to do that to me.
6. Refrigerate left-over gravy. The fats will solidify at the top. I usually discard the fat before re-heating.

Cheese Sauce

1 cup heavy cream
1/2 cup water
1 lb cheddar cheese
1/4 tsp Worcestershire sauce
1 tsp mustard
1/4 tsp paprika

Makes 12 Servings	
Analysis per Serving:	
Carbs	**1.1g**
Calories	221.1
Fat	19.9g
Protein	9.9g

Use a double boiler or place sauce pan into larger pot of boiling water. Add all ingredients, stirring very frequently until smooth (usually about 10 minutes). Serve warm.

Notes:
1. Makes about 3 cups. One serving is about ¼ cup (or 4 tablespoons).
2. This sauce is great over vegetables.
3. Add 1 Tbsp lemon juice to make a sauce for fish.

Cheese Sauce Mexicana

1 cup heavy cream
1/2 cup salsa
1 lb cheddar cheese
1/4 tsp garlic salt
1/4 tsp chili powder, optional
1 Tbsp cilantro, finely minced

Makes 12 Servings	
Analysis per Serving:	
Carbs	**1.4g**
Calories	249.1
Fat	22.9g
Protein	9.9g

Use a double boiler. Add all ingredients. Heat while stirring constantly until smooth. Serve warm.

Notes:
1. This makes about 3 cups. One serving is 1/4 cup.
2. This sauce is great over scrambled eggs, grilled chicken, grilled ham or almost any vegetable.

Cowboy Sauce

1/2 cup water
  1 tsp arrowroot powder
  2 Tbsp Worcestershire sauce
  2 Tbsp Nellie & Joe's Key Lime Juice
  2 Tbsp salad oil
  2 tsp liquid Barbecue Smoke®
  2 tsp Kitchen Bouquet
  1 pinch Sweet 'n Low® sweetener, to taste

Makes 8 Servings	
Analysis per Serving:	
Carbs	**2.2g**
Calories	39.6
Fat	3.4g
Protein	0.1g

1. Mix arrowroot and water until smooth and well blended.

2. Add remaining ingredients and stir well. Check for sweetness and adjust if desired.

3. Heat in sauce pan over medium heat, stirring constantly until thickened. Serve hot or at room temperature. Refrigerate unused portions.

Notes:
1. Makes about 1 cup. One serving is 2 tablespoons.
2. Try this sauce over grilled steaks, pork chops, chicken or even grilled fish. It's also makes a great marinade.
3. This sauce was inspired by Michael Annibali, I hope you know!

Creamy Dill Sauce

1/2 cup sour cream
1 Tbsp green onions, minced
2 Tbsp fresh dill weed, chopped
1/2 cup mayonnaise
1/4 tsp lemon extract

Makes 6 Servings	
Analysis per Serving:	
Carbs	**1.1g**
Calories	174.4
Fat	19.6g
Protein	0.9g

Mix all ingredients together well. Chill.

Makes a little over 1 cup. One serving is 3 tablespoons.

This sauce is great over fish or steamed vegetables. It's also good as a dip or salad dressing.

Cucumber Sauce

2 cucumbers, peeled & seeded
1 tsp salt
1 cup heavy cream
1/2 cup sour cream
1 Tbsp fresh dill weed, chopped
1 Tbsp fresh parsley, chopped
1 Tbsp fresh chives, chopped

Makes 8 Servings	
Analysis per Serving:	
Carbs	**5.6g**
Calories	153.2
Fat	14.2g
Protein	2.1g

1. Grate cucumber and sprinkle with salt. Allow to drain in a colander for 1/2 hour.

2. Beat cream until it begins to stiffen. Fold in sour cream and herbs. Press remaining moisture out of cucumber and fold into cream mixture.

3. Let sit at least 15 minutes to allow flavors to meld. Stir and serve.

Makes about 4 cups. One serving is ½ cup. Excellent with fish.

Green Chili Sauce

1 lbs pork loin, diced
1 can tomatillo, chopped
1 can green chilies, chopped
2 scallions, chopped
3 garlic cloves, minced or pressed
1/3 cup cilantro, chopped
3/4 cup chicken broth
1 Tbsp lime juice
2 Tbsp white wine
1/8 tsp Tabasco sauce, to taste

Makes 6 Servings	
Analysis per Serving:	
Carbs	**4.1g**
Calories	85.2
Fat	2.8g
Protein	10.4g

Brown pork in oil or butter. Add all other ingredients, bring to a boil. Reduce heat and simmer for 1 hour. Add more broth if it gets too dry.

Notes:
1. This can be used as a sauce over meats, chicken or fish. I like it over scrambled eggs.
2. Add another pound of pork and serve as a main dish.
3. Left-over pork roast can be used also. Dice the pork, add all other ingredients (eliminate chicken broth) and heat through (~5 minutes), then serve or refrigerate.

Green Goddess Dressing

1 Tbsp cider vinegar
1/2 cup mayonnaise
1/2 cup sour cream
1/2 cup heavy cream
2 cloves garlic, minced
1/4 cup fresh chives, chopped
1/4 cup fresh parsley, chopped
1 Tbsp fresh tarragon, chopped
1 Tbsp fresh basil, chopped
1 Tbsp capers
salt and pepper

Makes 8 Servings	
Analysis per Serving:	
Carbs	**1.6g**
Calories	193.5
Fat	20.2g
Protein	1.1g

Beat together vinegar, mayonnaise, sour cream, and half of cream. Stir in garlic, herbs, capers, and remaining cream. Season with salt and pepper, if desired.

Makes a little over 2 cups. One serving is 1/4 cup.

Hollandaise Sauce

3 egg yolk, beaten
2 tsp lemon juice
1 tsp sherry
1 tsp tarragon vinegar
1/2 cup butter
3 Tbsp boiling water
1/4 tsp salt
1 dash cayenne

Makes 8 Servings	
Analysis per Serving:	
Carbs	**5.7g**
Calories	143.1
Fat	13.3g
Protein	1.4g

1. Slowly heat and keep warm butter, lemon, sherry, vinegar, salt and cayenne.

2. Over a double boiler, warm egg yolks while stirring with a wire whisk, constantly. When yolk start to thicken, add 1 Tbsp at a time of boiling water, stirring constantly with wire whisk. When thicken remove from heat and whisk in the butter mixture. Serve immediately.

Makes about 1 cup. One serving is 2 tablespoons.

Hollandaise Sauce - Quick & Easy

2/3 cup mayonnaise
1/3 cup sour cream
1 Tbsp lemon juice
1/4 tsp paprika
1 dash salt
1 dash cayenne

Makes 4 Servings	
Analysis per Serving:	
Carbs	**1.2g**
Calories	305.2
Fat	35.2g
Protein	1.0g

Mix all ingredients well. Serve at room temperature or slowly warm. Careful not to get too hot or the mayonnaise will break.

Makes a little over 1 cup. One serving is ¼ cup.

Lemon Mayo Sauce/Dressing

1/2 cup mayonnaise
1/2 tsp lemon extract
2 Tbsp heavy cream
1 tsp Dijon mustard
   salt to taste

Makes 4 Servings	
Analysis per Serving:	
Carbs	**0.3g**
Calories	224.4
Fat	26.2g
Protein	0.5g

Mix together all ingredients. Refrigerate for at least 1/2 hour.

Can be used as a salad dressing or as a sauce over fish or steamed vegetables.

Newburg Sauce

3 Tbsp butter
1 cup heavy cream
3 egg yolks
1 shallot, minced fine
1 Tbsp sherry
1 Tbsp lemon juice
1/2 tsp paprika

Makes 5 Servings	
Analysis per Serving:	
Carbs	**3.0g**
Calories	269.2
Fat	27.5g
Protein	2.9g

1. Melt butter and sauté shallots. Add sherry and lemon juice.

2. Beat egg yolks, add cream and paprika and beat again.

3. Over medium heat, slowly pour egg mixture into butter mixture, stirring constantly until thicken.

This sauce is great over a crab omelet, steamed asparagus or grilled fish.

Makes about 1 ¼ cups. One serving is ¼ cup.

Oriental Dressing

1/2 cup vegetable oil
1/4 cup rice vinegar
1 Tbsp soy sauce
1 Tbsp ginger root, minced
1 garlic clove, pressed
1/4 tsp onion salt
   salt and pepper, to taste

Makes 4 Servings	
Analysis per Serving:	
Carbs	**1.8g**
Calories	247.6
Fat	27.3g
Protein	0.3g

Mix all ingredients together a chill for 1 hour.

Makes about 1 cup.

Pesto Sauce

1 cup fresh basil leaves
1 Tbsp pine nuts
1 Tbsp grated Parmesan cheese
1 clove garlic
1/3 cup olive oil

Makes 4 Servings	
Analysis per Serving:	
Carbs	**2.3g**
Calories	190.6
Fat	20.0g
Protein	2.2g

Combine the basil, pine nuts, Parmesan cheese, and garlic in a food processor and process until minced. With the machine running, slowly add olive oil, up to 1/3 cup, to form a paste.

Note: Since I use so much pesto, I usually just purchase the Safeway Select brand of pesto sauce. It's just as good as fresh made, however, this is not true for all brands of prepared pesto. Also be sure to check the label, some brands are higher in carbs.

Salsa de Cilantro

1/2 cup scallions, chopped
4 tomato, chopped
1/2 cup cilantro, finely chopped
2 garlic cloves, minced very fine
2 Tbsp olive oil
1 Tbsp vinegar
1 Tbsp lemon juice
   salt and pepper, to taste

Makes 12 Servings	
Analysis per Serving:	
Carbs	**3.2g**
Calories	32.8
Fat	2.5g
Protein	0.7g

Mix oil, vinegar, lemon and garlic. Chop tomato, scallion and cilantro. Pour dressing over veggies and mix well. Refrigerate at least 1 hour before serving so that the flavors can meld.

Makes about 3 cups. A serving is ~ 4 Tbsp.

Spicy Peanut Sauce

1 Tbsp peanut oil, or sesame oil
2 scallion, chopped
2 garlic clove, minced
1 tsp chili powder
3 Tbsp peanut butter, chunky
3 Tbsp water
1 Tbsp soy sauce
1 tsp lime juice
1 packet Sweet 'n Low® sweetener
1/4 tsp pepper
    salt to taste

Makes 4 Servings	
Analysis per Serving:	
Carbs	**4.9g**
Calories	112.4
Fat	9.6g
Protein	3.6g

In a heavy skillet, heat oil and sauté green onions, garlic and chili power for 1 minute. Add remaining ingredients and mix well as it heats. Add more water if it gets too thick.

This sauce is great over vegetables or chicken.

Makes about ½ cup. One serving is 2 tablespoons.

Tartar Sauce

1/2 cup mayonnaise
1 Tbsp dill pickle relish
1 tsp Dijon mustard
1 tsp horseradish
1 tsp lemon juice
 salt and pepper, to taste
 Tabasco sauce, to taste

Makes 4 Servings	
Analysis per Serving:	
Carbs	**1.0g**
Calories	198.9
Fat	23.4g
Protein	0.4g

Whisk together all ingredients. Serve immediately or refrigerate for 1 hour for better flavor.

Best with grilled fish but also nice as a garnish for steamed asparagus, broccoli or cauliflower.

Thousand Island Dressing

1 cup mayonnaise
2 Tbsp ketchup
1 Tbsp dill pickle relish
1/4 tsp worcestershire sauce

Makes 5 Servings	
Analysis per Serving:	
Carbs	**1.8g**
Calories	322.4
Fat	37.4g
Protein	0.6g

Mix together all ingredients.

Notes:
1. Makes about 1 1/4 cup. Each serving is 4 tablespoons.
2. Add 1 tablespoon of horseradish and this becomes similar to the MacDonald's secret sauce and is great spread over a grilled cheese burger (without the bread, of course). This sauce has 2.2g carbs per serving.

Desserts

DESSERTS

Cheesecake
Chocolate Decadence
Chocolate Mousse
Chocolate Mousse L'Orange
Coconut Cream Pudding
Coconut Macaroons
Cookies & Cream
Cran-Raspberry Cream Cheese
Custard
Dessert Blintz
Key Lime Delight
Orange Dream
Pumpkin Pie
Rhubarb & Cream
Strawberries & Cream
Whipped Cream
Whipped Cream with Strawberries

Cheesecake

8 oz cream cheese
2 eggs
3 packets Sweet 'n Low®
1/2 tsp vanilla extract
1/4 tsp lemon extract

Makes 4 Servings	
Analysis per Serving:	
Carbs	**5.5g**
Calories	366.2
Fat	34.3g
Protein	9.2g

TOPPING

1 cup sour cream
1/2 tsp vanilla
1 packets Equal® sweetener

This is a crust-less cheesecake. It can be served in a pie pan (double the recipe) but it tends to not hold it's shape very well. Ramekin are the best way to go.

1. Soften cream cheese. Beat eggs and mix into cream cheese. Add sweetener and vanilla & lemon extracts. Pour into ramekin (4 to 6 depending on the size). Bake at 375°F for 20 minutes. Let cool for 15 minutes.

2. Topping: Mix together all topping ingredients. Spoon on top of each ramekin. Refrigerate for at least 2 hours. Best the next day.

Chocolate Decadence

16 oz bittersweet chocolate square
2 packets Sweet 'n Low®
1 packet Equal® sweetener
1 Tbsp powered Greek coffee
1/2 lb butter, unsalted
8 eggs

Makes 12 Servings	
Analysis per Serving:	
Carbs	**11.4g**
Calories	383.8
Fat	39.6g
Protein	8.2g

1. In a double boiler, melt chocolate, butter and coffee until smooth (do not boil), stir frequently. Remove from heat.

2. Meanwhile. Separate eggs. Lightly beat egg yolks with sweeteners. Mix egg yolks into chocolate.

3. Whip egg whites until they peak. Fold gently into chocolate until well mixed.

4. Pour into loaf pan which is completely lined with wax paper. Freeze for 3+ hours.

5. When ready to serve, remove from freezer for a few minutes. Cut a thin slice with a sharp knife. Serve with 2 Tbsp whipped cream per serving.

Notes:
1. Although this recipe is higher than 10g per serving, it's a wonderful occasional treat for yourself without going too far over the top.
2. The bittersweet chocolate does have some sugar in it so be aware. You can substitute unsweetened baking chocolate and double the sweeteners for 8.5g carbs per serving.
3. If you can't find powered Greek coffee, then substitute instant coffee.

Chocolate Mousse

1 pint heavy cream
3 Tbsp unsweetened cocoa
1/2 Tbsp vanilla extract
3 packets Sweet 'n Low® sweetener

Makes 6 Servings	
Analysis per Serving:	
Carbs	**7.0g**
Calories	294.5
Fat	30.4g
Protein	3.6g

Add all ingredients into a deep mixing bowl. Mix with an electric mixer until stiff. Spoon into 6 ramekins. Serve immediately or refrigerate up to 4 hours.

Top with whipped cream, optional.

Chocolate Mousse L'Orange

1 pint heavy cream
3 Tbsp unsweetened cocoa
1/2 Tbsp orange extract
3 packets Sweet 'n Low®

Makes 6 Servings	
Analysis per Serving:	
Carbs	**7.0g**
Calories	294.5
Fat	30.4g
Protein	3.6g

Add all ingredients into a deep mixing bowl. Mix with an electric mixer until stiff. Spoon into 6 ramekins. Serve immediately or refrigerate up to 4 hours.

Top with whipped cream, optional.

Coconut Cream Pudding

1/2 cup shredded coconut meat, unsweetened
4 oz cream cheese
1 egg beaten
1 cup heavy cream
3 packets Sweet 'n Low® sweetener
1/2 tsp coconut extract
1/2 tsp vanilla extract
1/2 tsp almond extract

Makes 4 Servings	
Analysis per Serving:	
Carbs	**4.9g**
Calories	363.6
Fat	36.5g
Protein	5.3g

1. Mix 1/4 cup of cream with sweetener, extracts and coconut. Heat in microwave for 1 minute. Let stand for 15 -20 minutes.

2. Beat egg with 1/4 cup of cream.

3. Pour remainder of cream in sauce pan, add cream cheese and cook on medium heat, stir constantly, until cream cheese melts.

4. Add coconut and heat through. Add beaten egg, stir constantly, until thicken.

5. Pour into 4 small ramekins and refrigerate for at least 1 hour. Serve.

You can toast some coconut to sprinkle on top if desired.

Coconut Macaroons

1 cup shredded coconut meat, unsweetened
1/2 cup heavy cream
4 packets Sweet 'n Low®
1/2 tsp almond extract
1/4 tsp vanilla extract
2 egg whites

Makes 8 Servings	
Analysis per Serving:	
Carbs	**2.5g**
Calories	93.7
Fat	8.9g
Protein	1.5g

1. Mix the cream, sweetener and extracts. Add the coconut, mix well and let stand for one hour. If mixture feels dry to the touch after one hour, add a little more cream.

2. Preheat oven to 350°F.

3. Whip egg whites until it peaks. Fold into coconut mixture.

4. Using a teaspoon, place a small amount of coconut onto a well greased cookie sheet, making 16 cookies.

Cookies & Cream

4 Alpine chocolate cookies
1/2 cup whipped cream, sugar-free

Makes 2 Servings	
Analysis per Serving:	
Carbs	**2.0g**
Calories	168.3
Fat	15.5g
Protein	5.1g

Pile whipped cream onto each cookie. Serve.

You can also slice up 1 strawberry into 4th and put one slice on each cookie (before or after the whipped cream).. This will add only 2g carbs per serving.

Cran-Raspberry Cream Cheese

3 Tbsp cream cheese
1 Tbsp Knott's Light
    Cran-Raspberry Preserves

Makes 1 Servings	
Analysis per Serving:	
Carbs	**6.1g**
Calories	168.4
Fat	14.8g
Protein	3.2g

1. Zap cream cheese in the microwave for less than 1 minute to make it easier to mix (optional).

2. Mix cream cheese with the preserves. Enjoy!

Custard

10 eggs
1 pint heavy cream
1 pint water
1 tsp almond extract
5 packets Sweet 'n Low®
1 tsp cinnamon

Makes 4 Servings	
Analysis per Serving:	
Carbs	**3.2g**
Calories	302.3
Fat	28.3g
Protein	9.0g

Set oven to 350°F

1. Beat the eggs. Add all ingredient except the cinnamon. Blend well. Pour mixture into 6 or 8 ramekin dishes (depending on size). Sprinkle cinnamon on top.

2. Place ramekin inside a larger baking dish of cool water. (The water should be at least ½ way up the ramekin. This is what makes the creamy texture.) Bake for 30 minutes. Let sit for 5 minutes before serving or Refrigerate.

Serve cold or reheat serving in microwave for 1- 2 minutes.

Dessert Blintz

2 Tbsp Alpine Bakery pancake mix
2 eggs
2 Tbsp water
2 Tbsp butter

Filling:
8 Tbsp cream cheese
2 packet Sweet 'n Low®

Topping:
2 Tbsp unsweetened cocoa
2 packets Equal® sweetener
1 Tbsp water

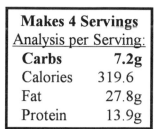

Makes 4 Servings	
Analysis per Serving:	
Carbs	**7.2g**
Calories	319.6
Fat	27.8g
Protein	13.9g

1. Beat eggs, add water and pancake mix; blend well.

2. Put a dab of butter in crepe pan or medium skillet on medium heat. Pour 1/4 of mixture into pan and tip so that it covers bottom of pan. Cook until slightly brown underneath. Flip and cook until slightly brown. Remove and repeat.

3. Soften cream cheese and mix well with Sweet 'n Low®. Set aside.

4. Mix cocoa with enough warm water to form a sauce. Add Equal® sweetener. Set aside.

5. Spoon out 1/4 of cream cheese onto blintz. Fold and roll like a small burrito. Repeat.

6. Drizzles chocolate sauce over blintz and serve.

I prefer these at room temperature, but they can be chilled or warmed before serving.

Key Lime Delight

1 large box lime Jell-O (0.6 oz-sugar free)	Makes 6 Servings	
3 cups boiling water	Analysis per Serving:	
2 cups sour cream	**Carbs**	**3.6g**
2 tsp Nellie & Joe's Key Lime Juice	Calories	167.3
1 packet Sweet 'n Low®	Fat	16.1g
	Protein	2.6g

1. Mix package of Jell-O with boiling water and add 1 tsp of lime juice. Stir well (2 minutes). Refrigerate 30 minutes (this is important otherwise it will separate).

2. Mix into Jell-O, 1 cup of the sour cream using an electric mixer. Pour into 6 ramekins. Refrigerate for 2 hours.

3. Mix 1 cup sour cream, 1 tsp lime juice and the Sweet'n Low. After the Jell-O has set, spoon sour cream mixture on top. Refrigerate or serve.

Orange Dream

1 large box Orange Jell-O (sugar free)	Makes 6 Servings	
4 cups boiling water	Analysis per Serving:	
1/2 tsp coconut extract	**Carbs**	**0.7g**
2/3 cup heavy cream	Calories	92.8
	Fat	9.8g
	Protein	0.7g

1. Mix large box of Jell-O with boiling water and coconut extract. Stir well (2 minutes). Refrigerate 1 hour.

2. Mix into Jell-O, 1 cup heavy cream using an electric mixer. Pour into 6 ramekins. Refrigerate for 2 hours. Serve.

Pumpkin Pie

16 oz pumpkin puree
16 oz cream cheese
 4 eggs
 8 packets Sweet 'n Low® sweetener
 1 tsp vanilla extract
1/2 tsp allspice
 2 tsp ginger
 1 Tbsp cinnamon
 1 tsp salt
 1 tsp cloves ground

Makes 9 Servings	
Analysis per Serving:	
Carbs	**7.7g**
Calories	235.7
Fat	20.0g
Protein	7.2g

Set oven to 400°F

1. Soften cream cheese in microwave. Beat eggs. Mix all ingredients until blended well. Taste for sweetness, add additional sweetener if desired.

2. Pour into a well greased (butter is best) 9x9 non metallic baking pan or 8 to 10 well greased ramekins (my preference).

3. Cook at 400°F for 30 minutes (ramekins) or 40 minutes for the baking dish. Serve warm or chilled. Top with whipped cream, if desired.

Note: if using baking pan, it is best to serve chilled (otherwise it dose not hold it's shape very well). Cut into 9 squares after refrigerated for at least 1 hour.

Rhubarb & Cream

1 cup rhubarb, cubed
2 packets Sweet 'n Low®
1/2 cup heavy cream
1/8 tsp cloves

Makes 2 Servings	
Analysis per Serving:	
Carbs	**5.4g**
Calories	222.4
Fat	22.2g
Protein	1.8g

Mix rhubarb, sweetener and cloves. Heat in microwave on high for 1 minute. Place in two small bowls and cover with cream. You can use whipped cream if you prefer but it will melt unless you let the rhubarb cool considerably.

Strawberry Cream Cheese

2 Tbsp cream cheese
1 Tbsp sugar-free strawberry jam

Makes 1 Servings	
Analysis per Serving:	
Carbs	**6.5g**
Calories	217.9
Fat	19.8g
Protein	4.3g

Soften cream cheese (zap it in microwave for ~10 seconds). Mix in jam. Serve.

Whipped Cream

1 cup heavy cream
1/4 tsp almond extract
1 packet Sweet 'n Low® sweetener

Makes 4 Servings	
Analysis per Serving:	
Carbs	**1.9g**
Calories	206.5
Fat	22.0g
Protein	1.2g

Make sure cream is very cold. Whip all ingredients together until peaks are formed. Makes about 2 cups.

Whipped Cream with Strawberries

1/2 cup strawberries, sliced thin
1 cup Lauri's whipped cream

Makes 2 Servings	
Analysis per Serving:	
Carbs	**4.5g**
Calories	217.7
Fat	22.1g
Protein	1.4g

Slice the strawberries very thin. Either serve the whipped cream on top or folded into the strawberries. Serve cold.

INDEX

Weights & Measures

1 teaspoon	= 1/3 tablespoon
1 tablespoon	= 3 teaspoons
2 tablespoons	= 1 fluid ounce
4 tablespoons	= 1/4 cup or 2 oz
8 tablespoons	= 1/2 cup or 4 oz
16 tablespoons	= 1 cup or 8 oz
1/4 cup	= 4 tablespoons
1/3 cup	= 5 Tbsp + 1 tsp
1/2 cup	= 8 tablespoons
1 cup	= 1/2 pint or 8 oz
2 cups	= 1 pint or 16 oz
1 quart	= 2 pints or 4 cups
1 gallon	= 4 quarts